LANCASHIRE
HISTORY MAKERS

Gordon Read

EP PUBLISHING LIMITED

This edition first published 1975
by EP Publishing Limited
East Ardsley, Wakefield,
Yorkshire, England

Text set in 10/11 pt. Baskerville,
printed by photolithography, and
bound in Great Britain at
The Pitman Press, Bath

ISBN 0 7158 1094 4

The author and publisher gratefully acknowledge
the following for kindly supplying photographs:-
City of Salford Cultural Services Department
(page 81); The Science Museum (30, 31); John N.
Merrill (34, 35); The Walker Art Gallery (46, 49);
The Bolton Museum (17); The Feoffees of
Chetham's Hospital and Library (25, 28); Lancashire County Library (7, 14, 90); The Editor of
Lancashire Life (18, 44); Liverpool City Libraries
(10, 20, 33, 50, 58, 59, 62, 64); Manchester Central
Library (23, 27, 38, 69, 71); Manchester City Art
Gallery and L.S. Lowry (85); National Portrait
Gallery (53, 66); Tassell (Carlisle) Ltd. (91);
Thomson House Library, Manchester (88);
Public Relations Officer, UML Ltd. (73, 74, 76,
78); and Wedgwood Museum (40).

Please address all enquiries to EP Publishing
Limited (address as above)

Author's Introduction

It is over a century since Espinasse produced his two volumes of *Lancashire Worthies*. Both volumes have long been out of print. Of the characters he wrote about, six are also in my selection.

Basically I have looked for people whose lives were both interesting and significant. I have aimed at a good mixture of types. All either originated from Lancashire and retained strong regional affinities, even though some moved away, or, coming to Lancashire quite early in life, made their contribution to history in a Lancashire context. All have been involved in significant historical or cultural developments.

To acknowledge my debts. As an adopted Lancastrian, I owe much to the nurture of the Lancashire Record Office, Preston, where I was an assistant archivist under Mr R. Sharpe France for ten years. There I first became fascinated with the many brilliant facets of this grossly under-valued county. From Mr J. J. Bagley of the Liverpool University Institute of Extension Studies I have received much wise guidance. Both Mr France and Mr Bagley have encouraged me from the beginning in this enterprise.

Of my three typists, Mrs Anne Coughlin has skilfully performed and endured most, without a complaint! Miss Mary Morris and Miss Linda Johnson have typed with equal skill and equanimity.

Specific help has come from: Professor A. R. Myers of Liverpool University, with ch. 1; Mr Hugh Malet with ch.5; Mr Frank Mullineux has helped me greatly with ch. 11 and checked chs. 5 and 11; Mr Malcolm Moore, Public Relations Officer, U.M.L. Ltd., Port Sunlight, has checked ch. 10. I bear sole responsibility for all faults and omissions.

To everyone who has assisted or encouraged me at all, I express my thanks. The Municipal Research Service of Liverpool City Library and the Lancashire County Library have been particularly helpful; I also thank the Director and staff of the Merseyside County Museums for much help and encouragement.

Gordon Read

Contents

Thomas, 1st Earl of Derby, The Lancashire King-maker 1435–1504

Throughout Lancashire one encounters the name Stanley, or the family title, Derby, on streets, parks and schools. The family have held estates in the far north of the county, estates in or near Liverpool, Preston and Manchester, in fell and plain. The 17th Earl was called 'King of Lancashire'.

Stanley is in fact the name of a hamlet in Staffordshire from which the family originated. Marriages brought the family to Cheshire. A particularly profitable marriage to the Lathom family heiress in 1385 brought a branch of the family to South West Lancashire. Royal service and favour raised the immediate ancestors of the 1st Earl to prosperity and prominence, including the Lordship of the Isle of Man. The 1st Earl's father became 1st Lord Stanley in 1456, dying three years later.

In one sense his son, born about 1435, was only continuing the family tradition of self advancement by knightly valour, service to the crown and judicious playing of the political game. This last was a difficult but desirable accomplishment in the slippery times of the so-called Wars of the Roses, (a title invented by Sir Walter Scott, the Red Rose in fact being the badge of the Tudors, and adopted by the County of Lancaster). Today's usurper was tomorrow's king and yesterday's traitor was today's liege man. It required considerable skill to defend the family motto 'sans changer'.

Consider the reigns through which he lived. He was born in the reign of the saintly but weak-minded Henry VI, founder of Eton and King's College, Cambridge, grandson of Henry IV, the first Lancastrian King, who had snatched the throne from Richard II in 1399. This violent act, though widely supported because of Richard's

Alabaster Effigy of 1st Earl of Derby with one of his wives, now in Ormskirk Parish Church.

misgovernment, set a bad precedent. Henry VI, who came to the throne as a baby, was dominated by favourite nobles and later by his bossy French Queen, Margaret of Anjou. Whereupon Richard, Duke of York, who also had a claim to the throne, feeling sufficient popular support, attempted a coup on the lines of 1399. He did persuade Henry VI and his council in 1460 to agree to his accession after the death of Henry. But he himself lost his life in a skirmish soon after. His son, Edward, though only a teenager, had all his wits about him and was handsome and gallant. He also had a way with ladies, which helped at times, but probably caused his premature death. No sooner had his father been killed than Edward marched from Wales and, after victories at Mortimer's Cross in Herefordshire and at St. Albans, reached London and was acclaimed by the citizens. He was also confirmed as King by the Royal Council. However, even after the battle of Towton, near Pontefract in Yorkshire, at which loyalist resistance was crushed, Henry and his Queen were still at large. Not till 1465 was he captured and put into the Tower of London.

It was the support of the Earl of Warwick and his retainers that had helped Edward to the throne. But Edward did not consult the Earl when he married Elizabeth Woodville. The Earl wished Edward to marry the sister-in-law of Louis XI of France. Edward, resenting the Earl's dominance, wished to ally himself with the up and coming Woodvilles as a counterbalance. He was the first King since the Conquest to marry one of his own subjects. Elizabeth's brother, Sir Anthony, was a renowned courtier, jouster and man of culture. He was a friend of Caxton. No doubt Elizabeth was pretty, charming and intelligent, but she was ambitious for her family to an extreme degree, even in an ambitious age. In 1470, therefore, the disgruntled Earl turned against the King he had brought to the throne. Edward fled abroad. The imbecile Henry VI was reinstated. With support from abroad however, Edward made a comeback. He defeated his enemies at Barnet; Warwick was killed; after a battle at Tewkesbury, Edward, Henry VI's only son was killed; Henry died, maybe by an assassin's hand in the Tower, so that now Edward IV was firmly established. He was an effective monarch. But on his death in 1483 his elder son, Edward V, was only eleven. The rivalry between the Woodville faction, led by the Queen Mother, and Richard, Duke of Gloucester, brother and loyal lieutenant of the late King and official guardian of the boy-king, erupted. Richard executed Sir Anthony Woodville, now Lord Rivers, and his nephew, Lord Grey. He put the two princes in close ward. He then declared the marriage with Elizabeth Woodville unlawful, the King and his brother bastards, on account of an earlier engagement of Edward IV, and himself therefore rightful King. Though generally an efficient monarch, for he tried to continue his brother's policies and sought popular favour by the reform of abuses and encouraging trade, yet he had alienated too many people in too many quarters. He never tried to scotch the reports that he had murdered the two princes. Lord Stanley's stepson, Henry Tudor, invaded the country in 1485 and defeated and killed Richard at Bosworth Field. This battle was a very near thing. Richard was a good soldier and had the bigger army. Yet it was on the allegiance of the great nobles and their retainers that the issue hung. Certainly the two brothers, Thomas Lord Stanley and his brother Sir William, played a signal part in deciding the issue.

Henry VII's throne was in reality far from secure. He had to suppress a number of dangerous rebellions. Sir William Stanley was executed as a traitor in 1495 for saying the wrong thing at the time of the Perkin Warbeck rebellion. Yet Thomas, his brother, steered a successful course between the shifting sandbanks, by a combination of luck *and* judgement.

It was no fun being a noble at this period. One might bask in royal favour and live it up one moment, but an indiscreet word or backing the wrong horse could render one worse off than a beggar. A peer was expected to give support to the crown according to his standing, pouring the contents of his coffers into the royal treasury in time of need and bringing armies of loyal tenants away from their lands in support of the royal cause. He was expected to take offices of state, which had invidious responsibilities as well as perquisites and might involve considerable outlay. In short, he needed a cool head, steady nerves, a well-controlled tongue, a memory long enough to learn by the errors of others and a heart not so tender as to grieve unduly at the fate of erstwhile comrades now in disgrace. He had to be able to profess loyalty in a way which carried conviction to the hearer without unduly stirring the heartstrings of the speaker, in fact in emergency to tell a lie without blushing. These characteristics, ingredients of success rather than of sainthood, Thomas Stanley seems to have possessed.

A 16th century ballad, if true, tells us how by steel nerves, he allegedly gained his knighthood:

> *When he was but yonge, just eighteen years of age*
> *The Scottes into the ile of Mann made a voyage,*
> *There did burne and spoile and did much outrage,*
> *But this yong man being of lusty courage,*
> *His father also aged and unwedlye,*
> *Had with him yong men a lustye company,*
> *Tooke shipping and in the ile of Mann arryved,*
> *Thought to venge those harmes or from life deprived.*
> *From man the wind scoured him into Scotland,*
> *And shortley after he had set foote on land,*
> *For to reward the Scottes with the same like light,*
> *He set on fire a great towne called Kirkobright,*
> *With five villages mo, or he away went;*
> *But since that tyme the Scottes in man never brent.*

'Good beginninge of a lusty ladde,' says the rhymer, 'the King to his worthie welcome home made him knight!'. He was to need his 'lusty courage' many times.

In 1454, probably at about the same time as this episode, he became one of the King's esquires. His first wife was Eleanor Neville, daughter of the Earl of Salisbury and sister of the Earl of Warwick, the King-maker, England's most powerful peer. But Thomas Stanley was, in fact, to rise as Warwick's sun set. Baronial diplomacy in this tricky period was much needed. Henry VI's leading counsellors, who had been at loggerheads, at his request went through a form of reconciliation in 1458, but the Queen, who had her own ideas, was not satisfied. A tiff between a servant of the royal household and one of Warwick's men led to a battle at Blore Heath, Staffordshire, in 1459. There the Earl of Salisbury defeated the King's supporters. Where was Thomas Stanley in this? The records say that the King had asked him urgently for help; that he had

promised it but delayed, excused himself and finally returned home; that he had also sent a letter pledging support for his father-in-law the Earl of Salisbury, though he himself did not appear on the battlefield; but that his brother, Sir William, a more impetuous character, had come to the support of the Earl, with a number of Lord Stanley's retainers, and that Lord Stanley had, by his mere temporary presence in the vicinity, hindered the King's Cheshire supporters from assisting the King's forces. Parliament petitioned for Lord Stanley to be impeached as a traitor. The King was no doubt soothed by Lord Stanley's bland talk, but the ballad relates an incident involving the Queen, who would have been less easy to deal with. Lord Stanley is said to have thrown his glove on the floor before the Parliament at Coventry, challenging anyone to charge him with disloyalty by picking it up. The gambit succeeded; the Queen was mollified. Parliament dropped the indictment. But Sir William Stanley was among those declared traitors. Lord Stanley took an oath of loyalty to Henry when he was knighted in 1460 and even delivered those connected with him by marriage into the King's hands.

Next year the tables were turned. Once Edward IV was definitely on the throne, Lord Stanley was appointed Steward of the Household and made a Privy Councillor. He had been Chief Justice of Chester under Henry and was confirmed in that office. When Warwick rebelled in 1470 he requested help from Lord Stanley, his brother-in-law. The request was declined, but when Henry was briefly reinstated Lord Stanley and the Earl stood beside the imbecile King. But when Edward returned, bygones were bygones. Lord Stanley retained his posts; in 1475 he accompanied the King to France, an invasion which was bought off by the gold of Louis XI. The result was an alliance between the two countries. To go on such a mission was a great honour; also acquaintance with a foreign king was handy if one became an exile.

Lord Stanley's first wife having died, he made an even more momentous second marriage, to Margaret Beaufort. Already 40 years old and twice widowed, she was descended from John of Gaunt. Her father, the Duke of Somerset, had been a powerful royal counsellor. Her first marriage, when only fourteen, was to Edmund Tudor, Earl

Lathom House, imaginatively reconstructed as it might have
been c. 1640, by E. Finden.

of Richmond, half-brother of Henry VI, and son of Owen Tudor, a Welsh adventurer who had married Henry V's Queen dowager. Though Edmund died in 1456, they had a son Henry, who succeeded as Earl of Richmond, and later to become Henry VII. But as yet, of course, he was not considered as a claimant for the throne. In 1459 she married again, to a son of Humphrey, Duke of Buckingham. After 1471 the hopes of the Lancastrians seemed doomed. Edmund's brother, the Earl of Pembroke, remained a staunch Lancastrian and took his young nephew, Henry, with him into exile in Brittany. Since 1455 Margaret had lodged in Pembroke Castle. On her husband's death in 1481, she was truly a lonely soul, with her only son an exile. Most other members of the once mighty Beaufort clan had lost their lives for the House of Lancaster. She was a strong character, indeed it was an age of dominant women. Her piety and cultural activities gave her relief from dynastic anxieties. John Fisher, Bishop of Rochester, her last confessor, in his sermon at her funeral said: 'Everyone who knew her loved her and everything that she said or did became her.' After her son became king, she patronized Caxton. She endowed St John's College and enriched Christ's College, at Cambridge, establishing the Lady Margaret Professorships at both senior universities. Among the young men who were educated in her household were Hugh Oldham, Bishop of Exeter and benefactor of Manchester Grammar School and William Smith, Bishop of Lincoln, born near Widnes, founder of Brasenose College, Oxford. Erasmus, who composed her epitaph, was an early occupant of the Cambridge chair which she founded. Her luxurious tomb, by the royal mason, Torregiani, can be seen in Westminster Abbey.

But these things were future then. In 1482 Lord Stanley distinguished himself at the capture of Berwick. In the ballad, Richard, Duke of Gloucester, King Edward's lieutenant in the north, is said to have left Lord Stanley to do the real work. It also tells us about hostility between him and Richard and between their respective retainers, culminating in Richard's threat 'by cockes bludd' to kill Lord Stanley and burn Lathom House, his main Lancashire residence,

on which he had spent much. There was a scuffle between the two sides at 'Rible Brigge' near Preston. Stanley was assured by the King that he would put his overweening brother in his place.

Next year King Edward died. Richard, his brother, as Protector of the boy-king, called a council largely packed with his supporters, among whom were Lord Stanley and Lord Hastings, the Lord Chamberlain. Perhaps Richard suspected Stanley and Hastings of wishing to obstruct his will. Hastings was hustled from the chamber by ruffians and executed that day, without trial. Lord Stanley survived a hard blow on the head, preserving his life, the London Chronicler relates, because he slumped under the table. He was put in custody for a while, but perhaps because Richard feared a revolt by the Stanley retainers, of whom, we are told by the ballad, Lord Stanley took great care in sickness and health, he was soon released. Sir William, his brother, was appointed Steward of the boy-king. A contemporary letter declares: 'There is much trouble and every man doubts the other.'

After Richard's usurpation, Lord Stanley, still Steward of the Royal Household, carried the mace and his wife bore the Queen's train at the Coronation. Richard sought to please the people, the Bishop of St David's writing that: 'Many a poor man that has suffered wrong many days goes relieved. In many great cities and towns were offered to him sums of money which he refused . . . God has sent him for the welfare of us all.' But less and less was seen of the young princes. Rumours of their murder raged at home and abroad. Meanwhile the Duke of Buckingham, Constable of England, who was keeping Bishop Morton of Ely prisoner, was discontented, perhaps because Richard had refused to grant him his family lands in Herefordshire. Morton was an old Lancastrian supporter who had become a confidant of Edward IV and had refused to accept Richard's usurpation. The Duke and the Bishop plotted a Lancastrian come-back. Perhaps the Duke, as Sir Thomas More says, had met Margaret Beaufort and heard her plea to pull some strings at court so that her son might return. However this may be, the Duke and the Bishop believed that if a marriage between Elizabeth, Edward IV's eldest daughter—the princes having been murdered—and Henry Tudor, now in exile, could be arranged, the union of the two long warring houses of Lancaster and York would attract popular loyalty. Margaret, now Lady Stanley, and Morton were in touch with Henry Tudor. He accepted the suggestion. All was set for a revolt by the Duke of Buckingham in support of an invasion by Henry. But Richard's spies were efficient and his supporters withstood Buckingham all along the route from his castle at Brecon. Henry sailed to the Dorset coast, sensed that hostile forces were massed to meet him and sailed back across the channel. The Duke was betrayed by a 'friend' and lost his head. Morton fled overseas to Henry. Richard, following Edward IV's policy of sparing the commons after dynastic fights, only executed a few leaders of the revolt. He hoped that clemency would settle the situation.

Lord Stanley must have held his breath. His wife, who was clearly implicated in the revolt, was deprived of her land. But they were merely vested in her husband. He, wonderful to relate, throve upon Buckingham's disgrace. He received some of his estates, and the Constableship of England. It is hard to see how he can have escaped suspicion. It may well be that Richard again felt that Lord Stanley was in too strong a position to be worth the risk of alienating him. He had such great territorial influence in both Lancashire and Cheshire and the fighting spirit of his tenants, as the *Ballad of Flodden Field* bears witness, was proverbial. He could put 10,000 men in the field.

In 1484, Richard's delicate and only son died. In March 1485 his Queen died too. Henry Tudor was consolidating his support abroad. Many people were deserting to him, the Earl of Oxford being the most prominent. Richard, finding his defence operations costly, raised the hated 'forced loans', a feature which both he and King Edward before him, had striven to avoid. He took strong precautions against invasion, for he had no idea where Henry would land.

Lord Stanley, his son George, known as Lord Strange, and Sir William Stanley were commissioned to raise troops for Richard in the North-West. Lord Stanley had hitherto been in the capital, close to Richard's eye. However he obtained leave to return to Lancashire. But

Richard thought he had a trump card. He kept Lord Strange as a hostage.

Henry landed at Dale in Pembrokeshire. He had only 2,000 men. No one obstructed him. He reached Shrewsbury without opposition; when Richard realised how near he was he had little time to gather his forces. Where had been his spies and guardians of the coast? He summoned Lord Stanley, who pleaded sickness. Lord Strange assured Richard of his father's loyalty. Henry secretly met both Sir William Stanley and Lord Stanley. Both probably avowed their support but thought that an appearance of neutrality at the start would be the most effective course. The armies met at Bosworth Field. Richard, who, in spite of everything, had more men than Henry and was the better commander, sent an urgent message to Lord Stanley to help, threatening to execute his son. Lord Stanley still delayed, but the exeuction squad refused to act, protesting that they could execute his son after the battle and no doubt thinking that if Henry won, with Lord Stanley's aid, they would suffer. Lord Stanley and his brother aligned themselves in an ambiguous position. Battle was joined, but they did not move. Suddenly Richard saw that his rival, Henry, was relatively isolated. He spurred his horse and charged towards him, even killing Henry's standard bearer. Just in the nick of time, Sir William Stanley intervened with 3,000 men, retainers of Lord Stanley and himself, turning the tide for Henry. All Richard's supporters fled, says Polydore Vergil, the Tudor historian, but Richard, though unhorsed, continued to fight fiercely, even madly! He had lost wife and son within a year. He had little to live for. He was determined at least to die valiantly.

Henry lost few men. He had to admit it was the Stanley contigent that saved him. Lord Stanley, says Polydore Vergil, placed Richard's crown, found in a thorn bush, upon Henry's head.

On the face of it, it seemed as though the forces of the Stanleys, by their inaction at first and quick action later, had put Henry on the throne. But it was equally true that people were not inspired with loyalty to Richard. Those he had commissioned to watch for Henry in Wales had let him slip through. The Earl of Northumberland had also refrained from action in the battle. The

London Chronicler, having described the despoiling of Richard's body and his burial by the Grey Friars at Leicester, concludes: 'If he had continued Protector of the princes he would have been honourably lauded over all, whereas now his fame is darkened.' He invokes God's forgiveness for his misdeeds. This is a fairer judgment than that presented by Shakespeare.

Richard was the first English King since Harold to be killed in battle on English soil, fighting for his crown. In the popular mind it was a trial by combat between Henry and Richard. God, the supreme adjudicator, had decided the victor.

Honours were heaped on both Stanleys. Lord Stanley became Earl of Derby, an ancient Royal title. He was made Chief Steward of the northern parts of the Duchy of Lancaster and Lord High Steward at the coronation. He was confirmed in his office as High Constable of England. He received the estates forfeited by the supporters of Richard and was a sponsor of Henry's firstborn son, Prince Arthur. His brother, Sir William, became Lord Chamberlain and a Knight of the Garter. He too received great estates which had been forfeited. After the Lambert Simnel revolt, in 1486, the Earl of Derby received more forfeited estates. But in 1495, at the time of the activities of Perkin Warbeck, who purported to be one of the murdered princes, Sir William was one of those charged with treason and executed.

Despite this, late that very year the Earl received a visit from the King and his Queen. The ballad-writer paints a graphic picture. Having told us of the unparalleled grandeur of Lathom as rebuilt by the Earl, he says:

King Henry the Seaventh, who did lye their eight dayes,
And of all houses he gave it the most praise,
And his haule at Richmond he pulld downe all,
To make it up againe after Latham hall;
To speake of his fare was sure so excellente,
The king and his company so well contente,
I hard noble men say that were of his trayne,
They thought they should never se such faire againe.
The king and all mused how he such fare did get,
They sawe never king have lyke chiere of a subjecte;
And each meale newe plate, they saw no more the ould,

Silver nor gilte, onlesse it were playne gould;
Counseller nor head officer was there non,
But the chamberpottes were fine silver each on;
The earles buttry and seller open night and day,
Come who would and welcome, no man was said nay:
After all such cheere yeat he gave such a thinge,
Was a princely gifte to such a noble king,
Pictures of all apostles he gave him all twelve,
Of silver and gwylte, also of Christ himselfe,
To parte with them would have made some mannes harte sory,
For they were each on a cubite lenghe and more;
In the jewell house who so liste to desire,
May se them if they be not hurte with fyre:
Thus is this king gon with honorable cheere,
Which was remembred after many yeare.
And propper Greenehoghe tower also he builded,
Which hath fewe fellowes all things considered,
Of pretty straunge fashion made all of free stones,
Yeat two lordes may well keepe howse there both at ones,
And the one not troble the other anye white,
So made of small compasse came of a greate witte.
At Handen and Knowesley made a greate reparation
And on Robert Rochdale was his free-mason;
Curstange bridge that standes on the river of Wyer,
Rochdale made the same on this earles coste and hire,
And Warington was kepte a commen ferry,
Which polled the people unresonably;
None might go to or fro on horsbacke nor foote,
But paye ere they past, there was no other boote.
The good earle considering the peoples coste,
And to make the way more ready to runne poste,
Being tediouse to passe by boate or by barge,
The earle made a goodly bridge on his owne coste and charge;
With another good substantiall purveiaunce,
Also gave landes therto for it maintaynance;
This was a noble harte, liberall, and kinde,
And people will praye for him tyne out of mynde.

He died in 1504, leaving his king a gold cup and legacies to various religious houses, principally Burscough Priory, where he was buried. After the dissolution of the Priory, his tomb was moved to

Lathom Chapel and Almshouses, near Ormskirk, built c. 1500.

Ormskirk Parish church. The ballad tells us about his bequests regarding bridges.

He was a successful man, but was he a good man? The ballad tells us how he helped people with lawsuits and taxes, but his riches and influence made this easy. Yet to a visitor who admired the mighty walls of his house he replied that he had an even stronger wall, the good will of his neighbours and tenants. Certainly the Royalist Earl, James, 150 years later, commanded an extremely loyal tenantry. It is appropriate that though Lathom House has gone without trace, the memorial of the first Earl's care and piety still remains in the attractive Chapel at Lathom with its medieval almshouses attached.

In his loyalty to the kings he served he was rather like the modern civil servant. Whatever king was in power, whether Lancaster, York, or Tudor, he served him dutifully *while he was in effective control of his kingdom*. Once Richard had clearly lost this control, he felt free to transfer allegiance. His loyalty was not to the King as a person but to his office. The Earl was no dashing knight of the old school, nor a saint, nor a humanist, but a great lord, a 'regional statesman' who knew how to be shrewd when others were rash and who, by his marriage to Margaret Beaufort, brought education and culture, just as by his personal success he had brought prosperity and prestige, to the people of Lancashire.

George Marsh – farmer, preacher and martyr, 1515–1555

The Reformation was a far reaching event in England's history. The breach caused by Henry VIII's 'great matter' would have probably healed in time. But the Reformation was a popular movement, the effect of which was to quicken the pace towards democracy and to implant a sense of national destiny. On an individual level, it stimulated self-reliance and independent intellectual inquiry. The wide distribution of the English Bible encouraged the spread of literacy.

Particularly in those parts of the country where trade was increasing, people were questioning the old traditions. The development of the Lancashire textile industry brought Lancashire into the currents of commerce that converged on London, the great melting pot of ideas. It was at London's wharves that bales of cloth concealing Bibles were unshipped.

Leland, in 1538, wrote that 'Bolton ... standeth mostly by cottons (not cotton as we know it today, but a heavy woollen cloth, probably with a linen warp) and coarse yarn'. The whole district was a nursery of Reformers, including men like James Pilkington, born in 1520 at Rivington, in a hollow of the moors north of Bolton, who, as Bishop of Durham under Elizabeth, founded Rivington Grammar School, and Thomas Lever, Master of St. John's College and later Archdeacon of Coventry. Their influence continued; hence the ecclesiastical historian Calamy could describe Bolton as 'the Geneva of Lancashire'.

Marsh was born in 1515, in the parish of Deane, near Bolton. John Fox, whose *Book of Martyrs* is the principal source, and whose general veracity modern scholarship confirms, tells us that he was 'well brought up in learning and honest trade of living by his parents' and that, when 25 years old, he married and kept a farm. Unfortunately his wife

George Marsh.

died quite young, but he was able to leave his children in the care of his mother and go up to Cambridge, probably in 1547. Cambridge was then full of new buildings. King's was barely finished; Trinity was just beginning to be built; Great St Mary's church still had the gleam of fresh stone.

Deane Village, near which George Marsh was born, as it was in
c. 1830.

Marsh was born about two years before Luther nailed his 95 theses to the church door at Wittenberg. Cambridge had long been a centre of Reformation thought. Erasmus had lectured there. Latimer was only the most striking preacher of the many which Cambridge reared. Some were martyred under Henry VIII. But, with the accession of young Edward VI, Protestant views were encouraged. The Regius Professorships had just been endowed. In 1549 the Divinity chair was occupied by the German theologian, Bucer, who, although mortally sick, delivered such passionate lectures, that John

Bradford, another Lancashire martyr, described him as 'God's prophet and true preacher'. His appeals for men of faith and disciplined life must have rung in Marsh's ears. No doubt he was among the 3,000 men who escorted Bucer's coffin to Great St Mary's. Marsh would have met plenty of old friends at Cambridge, particularly at St John's, the college endowed by Margaret, Countess of Derby, where James Pilkington was a Fellow and Thomas Lever, Master. In 1552 he graduated and received orders from the Bishops of London and Lincoln. This was so that he could be curate to Laurence Saunders, also to be martyred, who was in charge both of All Hallows, Bread St., London and of the parish of Church Langton, Leicestershire. There is evidence that Marsh and Saunders between them put plenty of work into the two cures. Marsh seems to have been occasionally able to return to his home district. With the accession of Mary Tudor, the reconciliation of the English church to Rome and Mary's marriage to Philip of Spain, the heresy laws were revived and the Protestant honeymoon was over. The Protestant ministers lost their

livings. Marsh became an itinerant preacher in the parishes around his birthplace, where, according to Foxe, he set forth 'God's true religion . . . by his godly readings and sermons in the parish of Deane, as elsewhere in Lancashire'.

Foxe's account of Marsh's interrogation, imprisonment and martyrdom is one of his best, full of interesting circumstantial details. He tells us how in March 1553/4 Marsh was at his mother's house when he was informed that Squire Barton was on his track. Squire Barton, a local J.P., lived

A room in Smithills Hall, where George Marsh was examined. He is traditionally said to have been examined in the 'green room'.

at Smithills Hall, a late medieval half-timbered house, which still stands. Marsh's friends were charged with the task of bringing him before the Squire at the Hall next day. This was the prelude to an examination before Edward, 3rd Earl of Derby, the powerful Lord Lieutenant of the county and a strong conservative in religious matters.

Foxe conveys vividly—he could well have had first-hand information from the martyr's relatives—Marsh's human reactions to the news; for he was no fanatic glutton for martyrdom. His mother and friends advised him to go abroad, like so many of his Cambridge friends. He thought of the feelings of his mother, his children and others, also of the almost inevitable consequence of staying in the country, the long drawn out judicial probings, foul prisons and the pain and horrible publicity of the stake. Earnest prayer and discussion with intimate friends, culminating in a sunset prayer-meeting on Deane Moor, a night of heart-searching and finally an unexpected letter from a friend urging him to 'abide and boldly confess' confirmed his decision to submit himself to examination.

His appearance at Smithills was brief. The Squire had the Earl's letter to hand by which Marsh was commanded to appear at the Earl's seat, Lathom House, next day. Hearing this Marsh sought that his brothers might not have to leave their ploughs at seed-time in order to accompany him to Lathom as his sureties, but he did not succeed.

They reached Lathom at the time appointed, then in its grandeur under that Earl of whom Camden said that hospitality lay buried with him. The fortified mansion was huge, crowned with towers, in which the Earl kept near-regal state, with his own council of gentry and clergy corresponding to the royal council, and household officers similarly entitled to the royal household. It would have seemed inconceivable that such a house could, in less than a century, be completely demolished in the Civil War.

There in the 'chamber of presence' Marsh faced the Earl and other Lancashire gentlemen, such as Sir William Norres of Speke Hall, now in Liverpool, Sir Peres Leigh of Winwick, near Warrington, 'Master Shirburne' of Stoneyhurst (now a Catholic College) along with neighbouring clergy, of which the parson of Prescot was the most loquacious.

Part of the examination was purely factual. Marsh was asked if he was a priest. He replied that he was a 'minister'—a name much preferred by Protestants—had 'taught a school' and that he had only ceased his activity because of the present laws. The crucial question, on which much of the debate hinged, was about the communion service—should the service be in English, did the elements actually change at the priest's words, and should both kinds be given to the laity? Marsh tried to put his case in a positive and conciliatory manner, laying great stress on the faith of the recipient as the vital factor. He was alternately coaxed and threatened, in order to make him either change his views or give a definite incriminating statement. He was patronizingly treated as a spiritual 'beginner' who would improve as a result of contact with the Vicar of Prescot. Sometimes his confinement was comfortable, sometimes not—a hard-soft policy. In his wish to be modest and not contentious he often feared that he was failing to confess his faith boldly. His key statement was:

My faith in Christ conceived by his holy word I neither could nor would deny . . . for any living creature.

Theological arguments failing, the 'ill-luck' of his fellow-Protestants and the present success of the other side was held up before him. To us today, with the benefit of hindsight, the fallacy of such an argument seems clear, but in Marsh's time, to all outward appearances, the life of Protestant communities did indeed seem to hang upon slender threads. Yet Marsh seemed to gain in boldness as the examination proceeded, despite false rumours of his own submission, and the groundless allegations he heard as to the defection of his fellow-Protestants.

The law took its course. Marsh was sent to Lancaster Castle, there to stay for nine months.

At some stage the Earl sent a personal message to Marsh while in gaol. Marsh, in replying, made the following points, namely that he had not broken the law, that he could easily have gone abroad and that the Earl had been one of King Edward VI's counsellors, therefore it was to be hoped he would not readily put poor men to death for still holding to what was enacted under

Edward. The Earl replied that he was a dissentient counsellor then and reiterated the argument from 'ill-luck' as applied to the late Dukes of Northumberland and Suffolk, two headstrong Protestant leaders in Edward's reign, who had both now lost their heads, as contrasted with the 'good hap' of Queen Mary.

During his imprisonment Marsh received many visitors. Some were friends and sympathisers, bringing encouragement and, often, practical benefits, among whom were the Mayor of Lancaster and the local schoolmaster. Others, meaning well, but 'without knowledge', spoke of various possibilities of avoiding the final issue. Marsh had little time for them. Priests also visited him, sometimes six at once, but all were either reduced to agreement or at least to an admission of defeat. To all who came, like St Paul, he spoke boldly about his faith, even to the judges, before whom he was 'thrice arraigned', with 'irons on my feet'. At his fourth appearance he was faced with a report that he had said that he knew many gentlemen in Lancashire of Protestant views and was pressed to divulge their names. After his vehement denial of this, he was 'threatened and rebuked' for 'preaching to the people out of the prison'. This was because he and a fellow-prisoner, one Warburton, held their eventide devotions 'with so high and loud a voice' that people sat under the gaol windows to listen. This, too, is reminiscent of St Paul's better known imprisonment at Philippi.

Eventually, came Dr George Cotes, the newly-enthroned Bishop of Chester, in whose diocese the whole of Lancashire then was, to Lancaster. He first took the gaoler to task for allowing Marsh such comfort and freedom to receive visitors, (by whom, also, the letters which Marsh wrote were conveyed to their intended recipients).

Soon Marsh was brought to Chester, to be examined by the Bishop in person. The key points were discussed again, the Bishop also stressing the authority of the universal church.

Other clergy came to reinforce the Bishop's arguments on this head, leading Marsh definitely to state his conviction that 'he did believe in one holy catholic and apostolic church' but that, to the outward appearance it was often 'a little poor, silly flock, dispersed and scattered abroad . . . led by the only laws, counsels and word of Christ, he being the Supreme Head'.

The final examination took place in Chester Cathedral. Civic dignitaries, as well as the Bishop's officials, were present. The main charge was that Marsh had, since January 1554, preached heresy in the parishes of Deane, Eccles, Bolton, Bury and elsewhere. Marsh, at this stage, stressed repeatedly that all he taught was that which was established in Edward VI's reign. This time all his answers were recorded by the registrar. There was no discussion. Within three weeks, Marsh was brought there again for sentence, and a last chance to recant. Marsh's answers on the earlier occasions were all rehearsed in case he had changed his mind. Then the melodrama of the reading of the sentence occurred. As the bishop read, the Chancellor twice intervened 'with a glavering and smiling countenance' and a great show of mercy to offer an opportunity for recanting. Foxe's picture of the scene, with the bishop removing and replacing his spectacles at each intervention, is almost comic. When the sentence had been read, the Bishop added: 'Now I will no more pray for thee than I will for a dog'. Marsh, undaunted, but still gracious, replied that he would still pray for the bishop.

From that point on, the secular power, represented by the City Sheriffs, took charge.

Marsh's condemned cell in Northgate was dark, bare and heavily guarded. Protestant friends communicated with him only through a hole in the city wall.

On 24 April 1555 the execution party, consisting of the Sheriffs and the motley crowd of armed barbers that was the city police, escorted George Marsh to the stake at Spittal Broughton, just outside the city. There Marsh was shown a royal pardon, under the Queen's great seal, available for him if he would recant. Marsh declared that, though he loved the Queen, he could never accept it upon that condition. Marsh's further words to the crowd were cut short by the sheriffs.

Foxe vividly describes the burning—the barrel of tar hung over the victim's head, the badly-made fire, flames blown by the wind, and the patience of the martyr in extreme suffering. Here, the effect of the martyrdom was, as so often,

The cruell burning of George Marsh, Martyr

Not upon ÿ Condition

George Marsh martyred near Chester, 1555.

merely to strengthen Protestant sympathies. The Bishop preached a strong sermon next Sunday, describing Marsh as a 'firebrand in hell', but soon after he died himself, owing, it was rumoured, to unchaste living.

From prison Marsh wrote several letters, to his flock at Church Langton and to friends at Manchester, Bolton and district. Of great interest is that to Jenkin Crompton and others in which lay people were urged to teach one another the Bible while the regular ministers were out of action. Foxe illustrates how this worked by his account of Jeffrey Hurst, a nailmaker of Shakerley, near Leigh, who married Marsh's sister. Though self-taught, and the eldest of a family of twelve, he became a keen Bible student. Fleeing into Yorkshire on Mary's accession, he used to return by night every so often, to visit his parents, his wife and child. He frequently brought with him a preacher and arranged a secret meeting. The local magistrates and priests heard of this. Foxe graphically describes the house search, while Jeffrey and the incriminating books were hidden under a vat! Queen Mary's death cuts the thriller short.

This is just an illustration of the deep popular roots of the Reformation and of the stuff both ministers and laymen were made of. Marsh's popularity is also evidenced by the fact that his name was long associated with a natural amphitheatre in the hills where he is said to have preached. The indelible 'footstep' imprint at Smithills Hall, where it is alleged that he put his foot down to emphasize a point, is likewise, though a legend, an indication of his local reputation.

In the 19th century an altar panel showing his martyrdom in relief was erected in Deane parish church and a monument raised on the site of the burning. Marsh would not have cared for these. What mattered to him was the faith he confessed and the firmness with which he held to it, as found and illustrated in a relic now preserved in Bolton Library, which may well have been handled by his own children, the Marsh Family Bible.

Humphrey Chetham, Merchant & Philanthropist, 1580–1653

Humphrey Chetham; engraving based on a portrait in Chetham's library.

Humphrey Chetham was one of the most eminent of the many Manchester men who worked hard and made fortunes in the 16th and 17th centuries. He, however, devoted a larger proportion of his accumulated wealth to the public benefit than any other. Today, Chetham's Hospital, now a school famous for its musical traditions, and Chetham's Library, one of the earliest public libraries in England, still fulfil his intentions. Dr Fuller, in his *Worthies of England* described him as a 'Masterpiece of Bounty . . . God send us more such men'.

The original buildings still stand near Manchester Collegiate Church, which since 1847 has been the Cathedral. Once the baronial hall of the De La Warrs, Barons of Manchester, from 1422 housing a college of priests serving the Collegiate Church, later owned by the Earl of Derby and in the hands of officials at the time of Chetham's death, because they were the forfeited possession of the 7th Earl, the executed Royalist leader, it was a double benefit, both of historic conservation and practical philanthropy that Chatham conferred when he requested that they should be purchased and converted to these charitable uses in his last will. The Library, which contains many fine books and manuscripts, including Chetham's own papers, still has much original furniture in use, so that the authentic atmosphere of a 17th century library remains. In 1669, Dr John Worthington, a native of Manchester, recorded that Chetham's Library was 'better than any College Library in Cambridge'. Till 1740 all books were chained. Twenty-four feoffees, successors to Chetham's friends, still administer both his foundations.

Manchester was synonymous with trade and was a phenomenon, even in Tudor times. Without borough charter or guild merchant regulating its trade, its commercial community was proud of its liberty and prosperity. A Manchester clothier, Sir Nicholas Mosley, born in 1527, the London representative of the family business, became Lord Mayor of London in 1599 and bought the manor of Manchester, of which the family remained lords till 1846! His epitaph tells us that:

> To Russe, to Tartasie, Fraunce and Italy
> Your home spunne cloth hee yearly made to see.

Leland in 1535 noted the imports of Irish linen destined for Manchester by way of the port of Liverpool. Camden in 1590 wrote:

> It has the best trade of any in these northern parts . . . Manchester surpasses the towns hereabouts in woollen manufacture . . . woollen clothes called Manchester cottons.

In 1641 it was said that Manchester merchants buy 'cotton-wool in London, that comes first from Cyprus and Smyrna and at home work the same, and perfect it into fustians, vermillions, dimities and other such stuffs'. The year following Manchester was described as: 'the very London of those parts, the liver that sends blood into all the countries thereabouts'. It was the marketing centre of the textile industry of south-east Lancashire.

Humphrey belonged to a family that had been in the textile trade for four generations. Born in 1580, the fifth son of Henry Chetham, he was probably educated at Manchester Grammar School; he was apprenticed for 7 years at the age of 17 to Samuel Tipping, his brother James' old master. In addition to his keep, he received 4d a year for his 'fyer and wages'. His brother George had been apprenticed to George Tipping, Samuel's brother, and had become a partner with him in 1610, managing the London office which dealt in 'stopport cloth, frizes, white ruggs and bays'. For a brief spell he became an Alderman of London in 1625. In 1614 Humphrey, after a spell in London with his brother George, became a partner with him. The business was described as 'buying and selling fustians and other wares'. The term 'fustian' covered a wide variety of cloths. The joint stock was £10,000, with profits to be divided equally. George ran the London sales, while Humphrey managed the 'buying and providing'

in Manchester and district. Humphrey would advance his weavers raw cotton and linen yarn, with credit for up to 6 months. He would handle the marketing of the woven cloth, which was sent up to London in packs of from 30 to 48 pieces, worth between 14/- and 25/6d each. Two to six packs were sent a week. The Chethams seemed to have been engaged only in the home trade.

Even by 1621 the brothers had enough money to invest. Land was the best investment. So they jointly bought the moated mansion of Clayton Hall, near Manchester, with its estate, from the Byron family who were short of cash. They paid £4,700. George Chetham died in 1626 and left various bequests to the poor, including black frieze coats to 50 poor old men and an endowment for two preaching curates in Manchester Church. Humphrey was now sole owner of the estate. In 1628 he bought Turton Tower, a venerable pele tower just north of Bolton which still stands in an attractive woodland setting. It had belonged to the Orrell family, but one member had incurred such debts that it had to be sold. Humphrey paid £4,000. He allowed the widow of the spendthrift to live at the Tower till her death. She was a Catholic, but Humphrey was a tolerant and understanding man in all matters. He even helped her with her tax demands.

In all his dealings he kept meticulous accounts. He was not only careful but scrupulously honest and fair. He was the principal buyer at Bolton and the story goes that when he had made his purchases there, one William Cooke, a less honourable dealer, took advantage of the situation, 'calling the pieces what length he pleased, and giving his own price'. Humphrey was very sensible of the social obligations incurred with his purchases of estates. He gave to the poor and towards the repairing of the local places of worship in the districts where his estates lay. He was also much involved in the affairs of the Collegiate Church, becoming receiver of its revenues. His practical and moderate advice and help was used in sorting out a corrupt Warden of the College, and in obtaining a new charter for it.

The fluctuations of trade were disturbing at times, but they were little compared with the upheavals of the Civil War, which were to cloud Humphrey's old age.

Chetham's Library today.

The principal complaints of the Parliamentary party were against the alleged unreasonable exactions of the King. This was what Hampden resisted. Humphrey was not of a reforming temperament, though no doubt there were many reforms he thought desirable. One gets the impression of a retiring personality, never so happy as when balancing his books. The secret of his success was no doubt partly business 'drive' and acumen, but also the capacity for steady, absolutely accurate book-keeping combined with incorruptible honesty, so that people of all parties and creeds trusted him with their trade and financial affairs.

Having plenty of money, he was an obvious target for State exactions. In 1631 he was ordered to 'compound' for not 'appearing at His Majesty's Crowneation' to take upon himself the order of knighthood. He was clearly the ideal person to be trusted with the odious task of collecting Ship Money, an ancient levy which Charles I found it convenient to revive.

In 1634 Humphrey was appointed Sheriff of Lancashire, the tasks of which included collecting all royal dues. He protested his unworthiness, but, of course, his lack of political aggressiveness and his scrupulous accounting were more useful to the hungry Treasury than gentle blood. Thus he was unable to escape the burden. He had to provide banquets for the Judges of Assize, including table linen, plate, venison and wine, he took out a coat of arms and equipped his entourage with a livery; also he was expected to distribute money to certain bellringers, town waits, and to the poor. He had to dress in unwanted style, gold lace, velvet, shoe rosettes, and a hat with a feather. Finally, he had to collect £3,500 in Ship Money. He tried to be fair, but it was impossible to please everybody. He spent much time dealing with complaints. However, he managed to get it all in except for a trivial amount. He also tried, with small success, to collect for the repair of St Paul's Cathedral. Despite his troubles, he received numerous commendations, on a private and public level, for his efficient and dignified conduct as Sheriff. A rare occasion of his expression of an opinion occurred when he expressed disapproval of the High Church flavour of the sermon preached before the Judges. He was clearly a Puritan in sympathies as in virtues.

Humphrey got into various petty legal involvements following his term as Sheriff. He also got into difficulty over his coat of arms. He was said to have appropriated that of someone else. Much interesting correspondence survives about this, including a letter from Norroy King of Arms certifying the spelling of his name with 'two h's and one e'. Humphrey from then on achieves distinction by being consistent in the spelling of his name!

In 1641 he was made a High Collector of Subsidies which were granted to the King by the Short Parliament. He did his best to collect the hated imposts. In 1642 Charles I raised his standard at Nottingham. Shortly after that Manchester suffered a short siege. The widows and orphans of the war victims were considerably relieved by humane men such as Humphrey Chetham. The Royalists who needed money found Humphrey as helpful in financial matters, even in the ultimate emergency of a 'forced sale', as the Parliamentary Committee did when they made him County Treasurer in September 1643. He was to receive all money collected for the maintenance of soldiers, arms, ammunition, even, it was hoped, for compensation for war losses, and to issue the money upon warrant from seven or more Lieutenants. What irony that the Collector of Ship Money should now collect for the champions of liberty from such exactions! It is the strongest evidence of his exceptional probity, for opportunities for self-enrichment in this time of confusion must have been great. £500 a week had to be raised in Lancashire. His total personal expenses on official business from 1642 to 1645 totalled £2,074. He hoped to get it back, of course. Some of this was rents paid in trust to Royalists whose assets were now diverted by Parliament to public use. Despite the infirmities of old age, Humphrey put much effort into collecting, only to be constantly pressed for yet prompter payment and given extra assessments to collect.

He had scarcely tied up these accounts when he found, to his horror, that he was nominated Sheriff again, for 1649. Worn out with his recent exertions and suffering yet more from 'age and disabilitie to travel', he found loyal friends in high places, and a fellow merchant, John Hartley of

Chetham's Hospital and Library as it was in the early nineteenth century.

Scholars of Chetham's Hospital dining in Hall today.

Strangeways, was appointed.

Despite official duties, expenses and the hazards of war and considerable generosity, Humphrey was still rich. He was a bachelor, and had made provision for his near relatives. Since 1642 at least, it is clear that he was thinking of an extensive endowment for the help of the sick poor, the apprenticing of poor boys and the keeping of poor scholars of local origin at University. In 1642 he approached the Royalist Earl of Derby's agent regarding making the College buildings a Hospital (we would now call it an orphanage). The buildings had been used during the war for prisoners of war, making gunpowder and its stone taken for fortifications. Pigs were finding shelter there. From 1649 to 1651 Humphrey's accounts survive concerning his keeping of 22 poor boys. He boarded them with families in Manchester and Salford and bought them not only clothing, but books including Testaments and Psalms, Latin grammars, and hornbooks.

In September 1653 he died, age 73, having been since 1648 largely housebound. At his funeral 40 blue-coated boys and poor men in black gowns led the procession. The funeral cost £1161! This covered not only mourning garb but much feasting. £88 was spent on 12 different sorts of 'comfetts', Naples bread, macaroons, biscuits, candied fruits, sugar and spice. 1,873 people dined. Much beer and wine was consumed; someone presented a sturgeon. Doles were distributed in most parishes of Salford Hundred.

The landed estates of Clayton and Turton had been settled in Humphrey's life-time. The value of his goods, including debts owed, was £15,130. He left £7000 for land to endow the Hospital which was to take 40 healthy and legitimate poor boys from Manchester and Bolton districts, and £500 to build or buy a house for use as the Hospital, preferably the College. He also left £1000 for books for a public library in Manchester, preferably at the College, £100 to fit it out, and £200 for 'goodly English books' for parish libraries at Manchester and Bolton Parish Churches and at Gorton, Turton and Walmsley Chapels of Ease. 'Godly friends' were named to choose the books. The Turton and Gorton Libraries still survive. It took much work on the part of his Trustees before the Hospital was eventually dedicated in August 1656. Very full records survive of the Trust's activities from the beginning. In 1665 the Hospital and Library were incorporated by Royal Charter. In 1675 it was decided that the Hospital Hall should contain a marble statue of the founder. This was not fulfilled till 1853.

But no doubt every one of the first boys in the Hospital could have translated:

Si monumentum requiris, circumspice.
If you seek his monument, look about you.

An outstanding historic building put to a worthy use accords far more with Humphrey's businesslike instincts.

Richard Arkwright, the first Cotton King, 1732–1792

Sir Richard Arkwright. (Crown copyright, Science Museum.)

In 1768 there was a notorious disputed election at Preston. Among those whose votes were disallowed was Richard Arkwright. He was in lodgings 'making a machine to find out the longitude' with the help of one John Kay. Yet by 1780 it was true that 'from being a poor man not worth £5' he was lord of a manor and had purchased an estate worth £20,000. At his death, aged 59, he left 'manufactories, the income of which is greater than that of most German principalities. . . . His real and personal property is estimated at little short of half a million'.

In the words of the London textile factor, Salte, Arkwright was a 'happy mechanic. In his lifetime he received the reward of his ingenuity. It does not happen in general'. This was because Arkwright had 'business sense' and 'drive', whatever else he lacked. To begin with he received great help, in finance and in technical know-how, from two established hosiery manufacturers who became his partners, Strutt and Need. In due course, though, he was able to stand on his own, to support other rising industrialists and become the prototype of the factory-master, in addition to his fame as an inventor.

In 1799 Arkwright's son tried to piece together his father's early life. The details are scanty. Born in Preston in 1732, the youngest of a large and poor family, he was apprenticed to a peruke (= periwig) maker at Kirkham, in the Fylde. He came to Bolton about 1750, married the daughter of a local schoolmaster, by whom he had a son, and began business on his own. He also opened a

The original model of Arkwright's Spinning Frame, 1769. (Crown copyright, Science Museum.)

public house. It was not a success, but he managed to settle most debts before he left the town, to become a travelling dealer in hair. But he was already well-known, in the words of Ridgway, the Bolton bleacher, for 'his genius for mechanics . . . we had often great fun with a clock he put up in his shop, which had all the appearance of being worked by the smoke of the chimney . . . . He was always thought very clever in his peruke-making business and very capital in bleeding and tooth-drawing'. He married again in 1761 a girl from Leigh. At Leigh Thomas Highs developed a machine which, it was later alleged, when Arkwright's patents were challenged at law, was basically the same as Arkwright's.

Spinning, though a domestic activity, was a highly-developed traditional skill. With the invention of the flying shuttle, and other aids, weaving had been so speeded up that spinners could not provide yarn fast enough. But co-ordinating the operations of drawing and twisting, which make up spinning, and doing both to just the right degree, was difficult. In the Midlands, two men, Wyatt and Paul, spent an estimated £60,000 to £70,000 between the years 1736 and 1758 experimenting with spinning machines. The machine was delicate and often broke down; the fibres often broke, too. Mechanised spinning remained a dream. The Society of Arts itself saw no future in it.

But the pronouncements of the pundits never deter true inventors. Hargreaves' jenny enabled weft (for the shuttle) to be produced in greater quantities, but required much skill for its operation and could not be adapted to non-human sources of power, such as horses or water. It was basically a domestic machine. The demand for warp threads, too, was still unmet. Highs was one of a number of men who experimented with spinning machines at this time. Perhaps both he and Arkwright were acquainted with Paul and Wyatt's work. Arkwright certainly knew about High's machine; he used High's assistant, Kay, who was a clock-maker, when in Preston constructing his machine 'to find out the longitude'. (This was to conceal its real nature). Thus it looks suspiciously like a case of invention-stealing. Indeed, in the final lawsuit of 1785, Kay and Highs both gave rather confused evidence, in which Arkwright was virtually stated to have done that. In 1823 Richard Guest published a history of cotton manufacture in which Highs was claimed to have originated both Arkwright's waterframe and the jenny of Hargreaves!

But in recent years an expert technologist, Dr R. L. Hills, Director of the North-Western Museum of Science and Industry, in Manchester, has examined the surviving drawings and the model submitted by Arkwright with the patent application in 1769, now in the Science Museum in London, and concludes that only Arkwright included in his machine two vital features, namely the correct spacing of the spinning rollers, to allow for the staple length of the fibres being spun, and the weighting of the rollers to nip the fibres tightly. Thus, though Highs, like Wyatt and Paul, had got so far, Arkwright alone 'reached the summit'. This is how things happen. One builds on the researches of another and the person who makes the final breakthrough catches the public eye. Highs appears to have hoped that one day, when he was in better circumstances, he could presumably patent and then exploit his invention. But, while he hoped and wished, Arkwright, typically, if slightly unscrupulously, learnt of his machine, hit on the vital improvements, with Kay's help, and kept the development dark for some months until at Nottingham, in June 1768, he applied for his patent.

By succeeding in doing all this Arkwright proved he had certain qualities that Highs, and other inventors, too, have lacked, which have been mentioned earlier, namely 'drive' and 'business sense'. He believed in his invention. He was able to persuade established capitalists like Need and Strutt that his idea was worthwhile—a vital step because the patenting and developing of an invention always demands money. Even after that there may be setbacks as well as external opposition, in the face of which the inventor must press on regardless. When these features are not found in an inventor he frequently owes his eventual success to a more business-like partner, as Watt did to Boulton with his steam engine.

In March 1768 riotous mobs destroyed Hargreaves' jennies in Blackburn. Hargreaves fled to Nottingham. Arkwright, then in Preston, feared the same fate for his invention. He had probably, as a traveller, visited Nottingham; he certainly was in Wirksworth in Derbyshire for a while. The hosiery industry in that district had long used a knitting machine, invented in 1589! Strutt himself had successfully introduced new developments. Here was a more receptive field for developing an invention. Arkwright's machine also produced a harder, smoother yarn, suitable for hosiery.

Arkwright's first partnership was with a Preston innkeeper and paint merchant, John Smalley and a Liverpool merchant, David Thornley, in May, 1768, as 'joint adventurers' to finance the obtaining of the patent and the development of the machine. This patent was not actually granted till July 1769. Arkwright rented premises in Nottingham, to which his two original partners moved also. But Arkwright needed more solid backing. This he got by his partnership with Samuel Need and Jedediah Strutt, to whom Wrights, the Nottingham bankers, recommended him, in 1770.

The Nottingham mill was horse-driven. A more spacious site with a source of water-power was called for. Hence Arkwright's machine became known as the 'waterframe' and the yarn as 'water twist' long after steam-power took over. A site at Cromford was leased, then a remote spot, with no turnpike road or water communication–though this might be an asset if spies or machine-wreckers were on the prowl! Arkwright's machine could be operated by a comparatively unskilled person. Thus it could use cheap labour, such as women, the poor—the benefits that would accrue to them thus were stressed in the patent application—and, more sinister, children. Now lead-mining, the old local industry, was declining. Thus in their wives and families, possibly in the miners, too, there was potential cheap labour. It may also be that Arkwright hoped to climb the social ladder quicker via the fashionable society of Matlock Bath than by the close corporation of Nottingham!

The whole geography of Cromford was changed. Substantial cottages for the workers, the Greyhound Hotel, a chapel and a church, all built by Arkwright & Co., still stand. The mill was five storeys high. Machinery was all constructed on

The House in Preston where Arkwright did his experiments in 1768.

Part of the original Cromford Mill as it is today.

site, clockmakers being vital workers. Lead mine soughs and Bonsall brook provided water, though later this proved quite inadequate.

One of Arkwright's few surviving—misspelt—letters, written March 1772 tells us much about the 'teething troubles':

I. . . . find no difficanty in getting it from the bobbin and dubeld and twisted in the maner you see it at one operation . . . I am sertain of ansuaring and one person will spin a thousand hanks a day so that wee shall want ⅓ of the hands I first expected. . . . I see greate improvements every day.

This is the language of success. The letter, written in haste, is full of business details, bursting with ideas. Clearly, Arkwright was the master-mind, at least on the 'technical and production' side. New mechanical devices were continually being added to reduce effort and increase production.

But this itself raised problems. A market was needed. Selling was hindered by the Calico Act, designed originally to protect the British textile industry. This Act imposed a double excise duty amounting to 6d. a yard on calico or cotton fabrics, which were originally all imported from the East. Now home-produced cotton cloth had

34

arrived. Strutt went to London in 1774 and worked hard to get the Act amended. He brought forward a draper who had actually substantially reduced his order on account of the high duties. The amendment was passed. Each piece of home-produced cotton had to have a blue thread and be stamped 'British Manufactory'.

Also, since all the spinner had to do with the water frame was to keep it supplied with 'rovings', fit empty bobbins in place of filled ones, and piece up the yarn when it broke, there was a great de-mand for 'rovings'. Once raw cotton is cleaned it needs 'carding', by passing it between two toothed surfaces to lay the fibres parallel. Thus loose ropes called 'slivers' are produced, which, when given a slight twist, are called 'rovings'. This is an example of the way the Industrial Revolution gained momentum. One process was mechanised; others had to be mechanised to keep pace with it. The letter of 1772 indicates trials of the carding devices. In 1775 Arkwright took out another patent, for ten different devices further to

The original part of Masson Mill, near Cromford.

mechanise cotton manufacture. Technically, Arkwright was vulnerable now. The drawings and specifications are vague, and the effectiveness and originality of many is doubtful. He clearly wanted to cover himself for whatever might be developed and had firmly grasped the need for a mechanised production line. That which is most likely to have been his, the 'crank and comb' device for removing cotton from the toothed carding surface, was, however, extremely important.

From 1775 Arkwright's mills at both Nottingham and Cromford were showing a clear profit. He built an additional seven-storey mill at Cromford and secured extra water in various ways. He considered steam power. But he had exhausted the possibilities of expansion at Cromford. He built two mills in Lancashire, one at Birkacre near Chorley, which was unfortunately burnt by machine-wreckers, who blamed the new machinery for the hard times, and another at Manchester, which was steam powered by 1790, as was the expanded Nottingham mill. Four more mills were opened in Derbyshire and a few in other counties. Arkwright visited Scotland in 1784. He was feted at Glasgow and Perth, but his partnership with David Dale in building the famous New Lanark mills was soon broken.

Seeing Arkwright's success, other textile manufacturers were envious and grumbled at the price they had to pay for a licence to use his devices. Patents lasted fourteen years or longer, if Parliament granted an extension. This income was bringing Arkwright great wealth. Some 'pirated' his inventions. In 1781 Arkwright unsuccessfully sued the 'pirates' over his second patent. He also tried and failed to get Parliament to extend his first patent and confirm his second one. The general opinion was that he had already received sufficient reward, in the fortune he had made, for his efforts. The verdict immediately set off a great expansion in the industry. He tried the law again in 1785 and won, but later that year Lancashire cotton manufacturers hit back, and not only brought forward Highs and Kay, with their stories, but stressed the vagueness of the specifications. On this count Arkwright lost his case. It was a popular verdict, in accordance with the traditional British hatred of monopoly.

But Arkwright's place was assured. His character was somewhat besmirched, but so is that of many great men!

Arkwright was, unfortunately, coarse-minded and quarrelsome, pig-headed and rather proud towards his partners and with his second wife. He broke with Smalley, his first partner, in 1777, and in 1781 Need died and Arkwright ended his partnership with Strutt, who seemed to handle him best, while fully admitting his faults. But, as a man of the people, Arkwright got on well with the people. Dr Neville, visiting Cromford, reports that Arkwright:

> . . . appears to know the way of making people do their best. He not only distributes pecuniary rewards, but gives distinguishing dresses to the most deserving of both sexes. . . . He gives two Balls at the 'Greyhound' to the workmen & their wives & families, with a week's jubilee (holiday). This makes them industrious and sober all the rest of the year.

Arkwright introduced the 'candlelighting' festival every September, with processions, music, feasting and dancing. In 1778 they sang:

> Our number we count seven hundred or more
> All cloathed and fed from his bountiful store,
> To our Noble Master a bumper then fill,
> The Matchless Inventor of this cotton mill.

In 1790 Arkwright obtained the grant of a market for Cromford. He provided prizes for the best stalls. He also sponsored a Sunday School and sick and provident clubs. The work force seemed contented, though the mill worked day and night in two 12-hour shifts. Child labour was used, but Arkwright tried to employ whole families together. It is worth noting, too, that Arkwright himself appears to have worked long hours.

After 1780, Arkwright had enough capital with which to finance others. His son extended this activity. The risk could be high. Their loans to Samuel Oldknow of Mellor, in Derbyshire, the muslin manufacturer who came near bankruptcy, reached £143,000! Sir Richard secretly lent £5,000 to Georgiana, Duchess of Devonshire, to defray her gambling debts!

Arkwright was a social climber, too, proud of his self-made success. In the Strutt family correspondence the style in which Arkwright and his daughter went to London in 1775 is noted and his purchase of a carriage—a status symbol—in 1776. He built a mansion at Cromford—Willersley Castle. In 1787, as High Sheriff of Derbyshire, he presented the loyal address to George III and received a knighthood.

Arkwright indeed had his faults. His refusal to adopt Crompton's mule, which was best for spinning the finest yarns, brought contraction to his business. Yet four great contemporaries witness to the regard in which he was held. Sir Robert Peel, 1st baronet, another even more successful cotton manufacturer, said in 1816 that 'we all looked up to him . . . a man who has done more honour to the country than any man I know.' The pottery magnate, Wedgwood, described him as a 'remarkable man . . . very sensible, intelligent' . . . and spoke of his 'admirable inventions'. Watt's opinion was that 'whoever invented the spinning machine, Arkwright certainly had the merit of performing the most difficult part, which was the making it useful'. Boulton, Watt's partner, thought that 'if Arkwright had been more civilised . . . and understood mankind better he would now have enjoyed his patent'.

Only because of Arkwright's inventions did the quantity and quality of cotton goods satisfy demand, as was stated in the House of Commons in 1779 when Arkwright's patents were discussed. The industry was expanding and exports rising. In 1775, less than 57,000 yards of British calico were produced. By 1783 the figure was $3\frac{1}{2}$ million yards! Watt's steam engines enabled factories to be more widely located and it became the key industry of the Industrial Revolution. Britain gained a head-start over all other nations and a new trade empire. Until very recently Arkwright's principles were still the basis of spinning and carding machinery, while the diffusion of easily washable cotton fabrics paved the way for the hygienic advances of the next century.

The Canal Duke—Francis, 3rd Duke of Bridgewater, 1736–1803

The Duke of Bridgewater and his Aqueduct, by T. Lowndes.

When Catherine the Great of Russia ordered her 1,200 piece set of Wedgwood china, painted with 2,000 views of English scenes, there was among them at least one showing the Bridgewater Canal at Worsley in Lancashire. Such was the fame of the work of Francis, 3rd Duke of Bridgewater.

Born in 1736, a consumptive like his six elder brothers, he also appeared mentally backward. For all that, after the death of his brother John, who had succeeded his father in 1745, he was sent to Eton, and then, at the age of sixteen to Europe for two years on the Grand Tour. His tutor-companion was Robert Wood, a classical scholar, author and pioneer archaeologist as well as a typical eighteenth century gentleman, who later became an Under-Secretary of State.

Along with continental culture, the young Duke saw continental canals. He may have seen the 15th century Italian canals; he certainly explored the Languedoc waterway, which links the Atlantic with Mediterranean. This work had been completed in 1681 after fifteen years labour. The 150 mile long canal section had been very difficult, but the project was largely financed by the brilliant engineer, Riquet, out of his own fortune. He died heavily in debt. However, by the time the Duke saw the canal, it had been profitable for some thirty years, enabling ships to avoid sailing round the Iberian Peninsula.

When in Rome the Duke also began his other great enterprise, the Bridgewater art collection, helped by a loan from Wood.

Having returned from the Continent and apparently recovered from his tuberculosis, the Duke began the life of a 'man about town', gambling and racing. He fell in love with the early-widowed Duchess of Hamilton, nee

Elizabeth Gunning, an Irish beauty. All was set for marriage, when suddenly the engagement ended. Elizabeth eventually married the heir to the Dukedom of Argyll.

The young Duke was upset, but sought relief in hard work. Social life he abjured for good. Canals and the prosperity of his estates, particularly his Lancashire lands, became his life.

The first Duke had taken an interest in the mines at Worsley as a source of income and in the possibility of a canal. There was a demand for coal and corn in the rising towns of Manchester and Salford so that there was a clear call for a more efficient means of transport to these towns. The roads were appalling. Wagons could often scarcely use them. The only all-season method was by packhorse, costing 40/- a ton, each animal being only able to carry about 280lb at the most. The Mersey and Irwell Navigation charged 12/- a ton, but the river was continually liable to silting and suffered seasonal droughts and floods. Despite all the work of the Navigation Company to maintain the river in a navigable condition, it remained in the words of the Duke in 1761 'very precarious, imperfect and expensive'. In fact an act of Parliament had been passed in 1737 authorising a canal from Worsley to the Irwell, but nothing had come of it.

The Bridgewater agent at Worsley was a remarkable man named John Gilbert who had been apprenticed to the firm of Boulton of Birmingham, jewellery and hardware manufacturers, later to become famous for their interest in Watt's steam engine. The Duke took to Gilbert from their first association at Worsley in 1757.

Gilbert was greatly interested in the coal mines. The perennial problem with the Worsley pits was flooding. The method of drainage used was the digging of a sough, or tunnel, into the side of the hill at a slight angle right up to the coal seam. The water flowed away down the sough. The early soughs were too close to the surface and always falling in. It was while Gilbert was staying in Manchester that he had the brainwave which ultimately led to the great canal enterprise into which his noble master put so much energy and money too, nearly reducing himself to beggary in the process.

Gilbert's scheme was to dig a sough well below the level of the old one and make it virtually an underground canal on which boats could float up to the coal face. This would solve the drainage problem and ease the transport problem at the same time. All the trouble of winching the baskets up the shafts would be obviated and the drained away water would feed the canal. It was just a question of raising capital.

The Duke was young, only 21, and Gilbert was 33. The Duke was game for the scheme, in one way a greater gamble and for far higher stakes than ever he had taken in his society days.

Only two years before, Berry, the Liverpool dock engineer, had constructed the Sankey Navigation which was virtually a canal which followed the course of the Sankey Brook, though in an independent channel, from St Helens to the Mersey. He was a useful adviser, but the Duke's scheme was for a waterway which was not dependent on any river course and whose water was supplied from the soughs and other sources.

But where to get the money? Joint-stock companies did exist, but the bursting of the South Sea Bubble had deterred investors. Fortunately the Duke had a vast and profitable estate, spread through many shires. He decided to treat the canal scheme as an extension of that estate, the loans being raised personally by himself and his agents. Along with money the Duke needed support in Parliament for the scheme, since an Act would have to be passed to authorise the many purchases of land along the course of the canal. The Duke was fortunate in having the support of his brother-in-law, the Earl Gower, of Trentham, who also had mining interests and, more important still, had brought him into touch with James Brindley, a Derbyshire millwright, with a flair for engineering who had actually prepared a survey for a projected canal from the Trent to the Mersey for Earl Gower. Indeed had the Earl been a little more daring he might well have beaten his brother-in-law to the title of 'Father of the English Canal system'.

Coal cost 10d a horse load at the Worsley pit head, but double the price at Manchester. It was surely time something was done. The merchant citizens of Manchester were quick to back the project. The Duke himself canvassed hard among the affected landowners. The bill easily passed

The Worsley Canal Scene on a Wedgwood Plate.

both Houses, whereupon the Duke gave a great ball in London, the last for quite a while. The Royal Assent was given on 23rd March 1759. The preamble to the Act claimed that the canal would be 'beneficial to trade, advantageous to the poor'. The Duke was committed to selling his coal at 4d a cwt. for forty years—about half the current price. No allowance was made for inflation.

The original scheme involved a junction with the Mersey and Irwell Navigation. The 'Old Navigators', as the Navigation Company was called, would not compromise over tolls so the Duke and his agent decided to adopt a more radical scheme which would compete with the Old Navigators in the carrying trade. Recalling the great features of Languedoc and the Martesana Canal near Milan, probably, too, the

Duke and Gilbert planned to build an aqueduct over the Irwell at Barton, take a branch of the canal into Manchester and swing south-west through Cheshire joining the Mersey lower down. The shaking mosses of Trafford and Sale would lie along the route. The Duke had certainly taken the plunge.

All had not gone well with the digging of the huge sough. The tools used then made little impression on solid rock. Nor did the idea make much impression on the colliers' minds. Finally they struck. The Duke graciously met the strike deputation, but he told them that quite apart from his canal, their employment depended on this work. The story goes that he took a pinch of snuff, held it up before the men and asked: 'Can you get that much powder from the rock between you all?' They admitted they could. 'Then so long as you can get a pinch of dust out of the sough, you should continue to work, and I shall continue to pay you.' Work recommenced.

Meanwhile, Brindley had come within the Duke's orbit. He, the Duke and Gilbert made a highly effective team. Brindley was asked to stay at Worsley Hall and bring his workmen to live in the village. The three men were marked by boundless energy, enthusiasm for civil engineering and capacity for hard thinking and hard work.

A new Act of Parliament was needed for the new scheme. No aqueduct had been built in England before. While the Duke and Gilbert concentrated on personal canvassing among the M.P.s, Brindley took on the task of explaining the technical details to the committee. Mere words failed to make the point, so Brindley, undaunted, took a whole cheese into the House. Out of it he carved a replica of an aqueduct. Still the committee could not see how it could retain the water. So he brought sand, clay and a can of water and demonstrated before their eyes that clay and sand mixed with water in correct proportions could indeed do the job. Even the Duke had wavered a little as he thought of the expense this novelty would involve. A three-arch aqueduct, with a three quarters of a mile approach embankment pierced by a tunnel for the main road was no light undertaking. An eminent engineer of the day called it a 'castle in the air.'

As an estate owner, the Duke could provide stone, timber, gravel and clay for bricks and 'puddling' (lining the canal sides to make them watertight). The rubble from his mines could be poured onto the bogs. The Duke took a very active share in the organisation of operations. Meanwhile his fortunes suffered from legal expenses incurred in settling compensation for land taken, as well as from the costs of construction. He reduced his living expenses to £400 per year, and his staff to one groom and one manservant. Even his carriage went. He was down to two horses. He sold and mortgaged what land he could. He even begged for small loans from his poorer tenants. By 1762 his total debt was £27,701—a colossal sum in those days. No banker would touch his cheques. Wages and salaries were in arrears. The Worsley mines were still not very successful. But Brindley's tenacity was an asset. As the three pioneers met at the Soldier's Retreat tavern on the edge of Trafford Moss, puffing their long clay pipes, Brindley terminated their fruitless deliberations about where to raise more money with the remark: 'Don't mind, Duke, don't be cast down; we're sure to succeed after all!' Whereupon he rode off on his famous mare to continue with forward operations which were his responsibility.

Work on the great aqueduct across the Irwell began even before the second Act was passed. As satisfactory progress was made, generous allowances of ale were made to all concerned. The surviving accounts also revealed that provision was made for sick or injured workers.

Snags were encountered but overcome; economies were devised, but it was a tense time, waiting for the aqueduct to be completed. It was a race against mounting debt, with vast interest, and sinking credit. At last Brindley claimed that the aqueduct would take the water. As water flowed in, those watching held their breath. Alas, one arch showed signs of weakness. Poor Brindley, worn out with work and worry, had a breakdown. The trouble was that the sides of the arch bore too much weight. The resourceful Gilbert removed the clay, covered the stone work of the arch with straw to prevent slipping and put on a fresh lining of clay. It worked!

On 17th July, 1761 a barge carrying 50 tons of coal was towed towards Manchester. A party of gentry, including the Duke's friend the Earl of Stamford, who had large estates nearby, watched the inaugural demonstration. Overnight Barton-on-Irwell had become the site of one of the wonders of the world. It became a fashionable place to visit. The arches rose 39 feet above the Irwell bed, the mass of masonry was 250 feet long and 36 feet wide. What amazed people so much was that no water oozed through it. The outer stonework later had to be refaced, but a small part of it is still standing today, the greater part having, unfortunately, been demolished to make way for the Manchester Ship Canal.

Thus at the age of twenty five, the Duke was a national hero. So were Gilbert and Brindley. The Duke was vindicated in the minds of the investing public, too. But coal and agricultural produce sold at Manchester would not clear his debts soon enough. If he could only build the stretch through Cheshire to Runcorn, he would reap the rewards of the carrying trade from Manchester to Liverpool. But money was needed. Furthermore, the Old Navigators had had time to rally their ranks.

The Duke had been skilful. In obtaining his earlier acts, he had merely sought the powers needed for immediate objectives, while the grand design still lay in his and his two colleagues' minds. Now, having achieved what they had been told was physically impossible, they were ready to try the morally impossible, namely, to extend a canal that would break the trade monopoly of the Mersey and Irwell Navigators!

Opposition had indeed hardened in the House. Once the Duke had revealed his full plan, it became a party issue. Generally the Tories supported the Old Navigators and the obstructors, while the Whigs supported the Duke and progress. After all, newly cut canals disfigured the countryside for a long time, before grass grew again on the banks. Landowners could stick out for a high price, too. This sort of opposition prevented the canal from reaching the centre of Manchester for some years.

The Old Navigators' arguments were first, that the canal would steal their water. The Duke contended that his water would come from mine soughs and brought the great lighthouse engineer, Smeaton, to join with Brindley in confirmation of his calculations. Secondly, it was urged that the Old Navigation had not yet begun to pay its way, and therefore there could not be enough trade for both it and the canal. In fact it was claimed that parliament had granted them a monopoly. The Duke was able to turn this argument. Because the Old Navigation was inefficient and unprofitable he asked, was he to refrain from an enterprise that would be both efficient and immune from the vagaries of floods, tides and shoals? Why should he not carry for 6/- a ton, merely because he would undersell the Old Navigators whose price was 12/-? The opposition had overplayed its hand. Popular feeling was against monopoly, and in this case its instinct was right, for monopoly is a hindrance to that individual initiative upon which progress depends.

When in London on the business of his third Act, the Duke stayed with his mother and the step-father whom he had so disliked as a boy. By now they saw they had misjudged the young Francis.

The Duke's painstaking canvassing and the weight of expert witnesses won the day in Parliament. He hastened to press on. The Worsley to Manchester waterway was just ten miles long. The new stretch was more than twice as long. Despite the extra cost, the Duke wisely kept to his original broad gauge of 14 feet. It was to follow the level north of Altrincham through Lymm and a little south of Warrington, to be locked down to the Mersey near Runcorn by ten locks. Again, the Duke committed himself to low tolls, 6/- a ton for carriage between Manchester and Liverpool.

The problems were the same as before, but multiplied. Even small landholders stood on their rights, like an old crofter, who got £30 for a small garden with only one old pear tree in it. In Runcorn the Duke was forced to pay up to £40,000 for one acre! He sometimes had to bend the canal's course to avoid an awkward landowner's territory.

Progress continued on three fronts at once. Soughs were still being driven underground at Worsley, which became an inland port. At Manchester a loading terminus was being built on the site of the Roman fort. A sough was even drilled under the little hill there and coal was winched up the shafts at the end of it by water-power, to be dumped right at the feet of the customers. Brindley had to build a wooden case to take the canal through the worst part of Sale Moss. By 1763 the other aqueduct, that at Stretford, across the Mersey, had been finished.

The leisure potential of the canal was seen early. The Earl of Stamford built himself a bathing house and a harbour for a pleasure boat. The Duke himself exploited the canal and even the gloomy soughs as a tourist attraction. Visitors included the philosopher Rousseau and King Christian VI of Denmark. Parties went up the sough in special narrow boats equipped with candles. Handsome tips for the workmen as well as admiration were forthcoming from rich visitors. The first passenger boats plied in 1766, with first and second class accommodation and refreshments. Fast horses drew them to fixed timetables at a charge of 1d a mile.

Visitors to the soughs compared their experiences with the underworld of classical mythology. Wine was provided to revive the faint. Doors at the tunnel mouth closed eerily behind the boats. Work in the mines was not suspended. The grating of winches, the roar of blasting, and songs of male and female mine workers met the ear. When the head of the mine was reached the work force could be seen 'almost in their primitive state of nature' as one visitor neatly put it!

By 1765 the mines were quite profitable, but the canal debt was over £60,000. The Duke's credit was higher now, but a £25,000 loan from Childs, the family bank, did not go far. But he continued to honour his statutory pledge. He sold coals at 3½d a cwt., at Manchester till 1793, when inflation of wages made him raise it to 4½d.

Another cloud was coming over the Duke's horizon in the shape of rival schemes. A Trent-Mersey canal was being considered, to join the River Weaver, a tributary of the Mersey. Brindley had been engaged by Josiah Wedgwood, now a leading promoter. The Duke realised that it was vital for this new canal to connect with his. He invited Wedgwood to Worsley in July 1765. The two great entrepreneurs had much in common. Wedgwood enjoyed his nine mile sail 'thro' a most delightful vale' to Manchester by 'gondola'. The impoverished Duke ordered a complete table service of cream ware costing £160, but worth it for goodwill! Wedgwood became his ally. The Trent and Mersey Canal was to end at Preston Brook in Cheshire where it would join the Duke's canal. The Duke was to be a leading shareholder in Wedgwood's scheme.

By 1771 the Duke's debt was more than double that what it was in 1765 and for three years now he had been fighting the most reactionary landlord he had ever met, namely, Sir Richard Brooke of Norton Priory, an estate which lay right athwart the approach to Runcorn. For seven years Sir Richard held out asking fantastic prices and rallying support. But the canal promoters were not cowed. Having paid so heavily for the dock estate at Runcorn, they pressed on with wharves and warehouses and began work on the ten locks. It was over the Runcorn lock that the Duke and Brindley disagreed and parted company. The three colleagues, the Duke, Gilbert and Brindley, had met to discuss technicalities. The Duke held his point and events proved him right.

Brindley, however, had many other commitments to get on with. He also had a young wife—he married at 49 to an eighteen year old girl—and soon after bought a small estate, took out a coat of arms and entered the ranks of the landed gentry, only to die of diabetes in 1772 at the age of 56.

The crucial flight of ten locks at Runcorn was finished in 1773. Like pincers the two lengths of waterway beset Sir Richard Brooke on either side. The Duke inaugurated the opening of the Runcorn stretch with great eclat, entertaining over 600 workmen with whole roast ox and ale, while a fifty ton boat passed along the canal bound for Liverpool. The Duke had still to unship goods where the canal stopped at Norton Priory boundary and carry them overland to other vessels waiting near the locks. The cost of this delay increased the pressure upon Sir Richard. Suddenly the opposition collapsed. Sir Richard compromised. Work recommenced and by 21st March 1776 the link was complete. The Duke had won.

But the canal had not yet begun to pay. Maintenance and improvements were needed. The highest point of debt was in 1786, when it reached £346,805. However his canal profits were then over £17,000 which virtually cleared the interest.

Although trade fluctuated and thus the canal sometimes made a loss the Duke never looked back. Not till many years after the Duke's death in 1803, was the debt totally cleared, however.

What sort of man was the Duke? Clearly he had an engineer's mind and a will to succeed. He was also somewhat eccentric. He usually wore a shabby outdated brown coat and breeches, stained with snuff. He usually spoke broad Lancashire and never moderated his language for ladies! He supervised the activities of the canal personally, checked the accounts himself, helped customers with their loads and never stood on ceremony.

He was also an efficient farmer. He tried to reclaim wastes such as Chat Moss and consequently, Arthur Young, the travelling agriculturist, paid him special tribute.

The Packet House, Worsley, as it is today.

The Duke had a kind heart. The accountant at his Manchester wharves was instructed to reserve an adequate supply of coal for the poorer people however short it might be. No wonder that Manchester crowds cheered him in the streets one day. When in 1783 the Duke felt his financial position easier he ordered bonuses for his mine workers. Normally colliers were fined 2/6d for lateness to work, but when the Duke met one latecomer, hearing that the man's wife had produced twins in the night, he gave him a guinea instead. His welfare schemes were reported on by the Society for Bettering the Conditions of the Poor. He let subsidised housing and ran a canteen. Estate shopkeepers were instructed to charge reasonable prices. Heavy drinking was discouraged, though the Duke frequently treated his men on days of celebration. He paid for medical attention and ran a sick club whose members included his own agent as well as colliers. Sunday schools and even a floating church-in-a-barge were provided. So much for his reputed lack of religion.

He was constantly experimenting, and became, even near the end of his life time, interested in steam propulsion of boats, and an experimental boat, called *Buonaparte,* was tried. It only travelled at 1 m.p.h.! For the Duke, Gilbert devised an inclined plane for joining the two levels of sough in his mines. A loaded boat slid down pulling an empty one up at the same time. For this the Duke was awarded a gold medal by the Society of Arts.

As he defrayed his debts, he bought a carriage again. It eased his gout when travelling. By 1794 he had time to resume collecting pictures, the hobby of his youth. His collection became famous. He patronised Turner generously. He began collecting books, too. He gave Brindley a prayer book which its receiver always treasured. He also subscribed to a set of Bibles with commentary.

He has been accused of meanness, particularly towards Brindley. But he gave Brindley his keep as well as his pay. Also Brindley, like Gilbert, was free to develop business on the side. The Duke's neighbour, Hulbert, reported that if one could become a tenant of the Duke one was thought fortunate. His name was a local byword for kindly virtues.

His works at Worsley can still be seen. But in one sense all the canals in England are his monument.

William Roscoe, Man of Parts, 1753–1831

William Roscoe at Holkham Hall, 1822. This picture, by Sir M. A. Shee, shows Roscoe among the manuscripts in 'Coke of Norfolk's' Library.

To write major works on Lorenzo de Medici and Pope Leo X, lead the local movement against the slave trade, become widely known as a botanist, poet, collector and patron of the arts, sit in Parliament, be an experimental farmer, edit the works of Alexander Pope, run a successful legal practice, become a merchant banker by the way, rear a large family successfully, catalogue a world famous collection of rare manuscripts and campaign for penal reform was the achievement of one man, a native and life-long citizen of Liverpool who rarely went far from his native town and never left his native land. Truly a man of parts. His name was William Roscoe.

The rising seaport town into which Roscoe was born in 1753 had then a population of 21,000. It was a fairly large town for its time, but without any cultural pretensions. Even in 1795 it could be described as 'a remote commercial town where nothing is heard of but Guinea ships, slaves, blacks and merchandise'.

Roscoe's father kept an inn, the Old Bowling Green. William left school at the age of twelve and devoted himself to helping his father in growing and selling early potatoes and other vegetables. This involved carrying full baskets to market on his head. From this aspect of his youth he derived his love of the soil and of nature. His love of poetry he imbibed, he says, from his mother. Liverpool had one artistic tradition, that of figured pottery; he learned painting from the artists of Reid's china works next to his father's market garden. He was an avid reader. It was this feature that led his father to find him a job with John Gore, the local bookseller, at the age of fifteen. Congenial as this may have been, after one month he became articled to a local solicitor for a six year term.

But another side than the cultural was being formed in his character. This was an age of cruel sports. Cock-fighting, bull- and bear-baiting were in vogue with all classes. Only a few Nonconformists and members of the Society of Friends stood out against popular taste. But Roscoe was a sensitive soul. Out shooting once, he maimed a bird and was so upset that he never shot again. His mother's early death impressed her sensitive life-view on his mind. While in articles, too, he lodged with a retired slave captain, who drank himself to death. Thus the foundations were laid for a life not only of devotion to the fine arts but to all humane causes.

All this was reinforced by Roscoe's Nonconformist creed. He was a Presbyterian. By then most Presbyterians had become Unitarians. Though less definite in doctrine, they still retained the Nonconformist conscience, in fact, their creed was mainly a social and cultural one. The Nonconformist ministers and laymen provided a strong cultural and social 'lobby' in the town and district.

Roscoe's life was thus to be a combination of patronage of the arts and sciences and championship of liberty with business activity, first as a lawyer, land investor, and finally banker, all highly successful until the unfortunate bankruptcy of 1816. It was impossible for him to be a single-minded professional man.

In his early poem, *Mount Pleasant*, written in 1771, he asked:

Ah! why ye sons of wealth with ceaseless toil
Add gold to gold, and swell the shining pile?

The poem is basically a series of reflections stimulated by the view from his native hill which was called Mount Pleasant. The view of the estuary, then unobscured by blocks of flats, must have been highly pleasing. The Mersey, then unpolluted, would be alive with bobbing masts and sails.

The sight of the many new buildings Liverpool's thriving trade had helped to rear and the vast concourse of shipping led him to reflect sadly on the philistinism and the ruthless exploitation of black Africans which marked these merchants:

Shame to mankind! But shame to Britons most,
Who all the sweets of liberty can boast;
Yet, deaf to every human claim, deny
That bliss to others, which themselves enjoy.

though he noted more favourably the Theatre and charity buildings.

It is easy to snigger at the trite observations of which Roscoe's verse was so full. In their time, though, the poems were much admired even by London critics. Indeed, Liverpool became famous for poetry on Roscoe's account. It was his very absorption with the classical poets of his youth, particularly with Pope, whom he much admired, which fossilized his poetic talent. At all life's junctures, courtship and married life, political crises and calls for compassion Roscoe broke into verse.

Yet Roscoe not only personally studied the English classics, but joined a local group of young intellectuals which met before work, early in the morning, to study Latin and Italian.

Roscoe was thoroughly human, falling in love at an early age, before his articles were out. In 1781 he married, happily and fruitfully:

Six sons successive, and ...
Two Daughters fair.

Ultimately he had seven sons and three daughters. The poem just quoted entitled *Sonnet to Mrs Roscoe* prefaced his translation of the work of the Italian poet Tansillo, entitled *The Nurse*, written to encourage upper-class women to suckle their own children, a cause Roscoe eagerly took up. The current practice of wet-nursing, which interposed another woman between mother and child at a formative age, he heartily deplored.

He made his wife and family the excuse for not travelling abroad, despite his wide range of interests. His ill success as an M.P. can in part be explained by the fact that he missed his wife. His sons and daughters shared their father's interests, and, to some degree, his talents, In all, the family must have provided a cultured domestic circle, with unrepressed and genuine affection. It is no wonder, then, that probably Roscoe's best poem was one written for his son Robert, *The Butterfly's Ball and the Grasshopper's Feast*.

It was a great success, like most of his poems. George III and his Queen heard of it, liked it and had it set to music for the young princesses. For once Roscoe avoids the pointed moral and the overweight of classical cliches. There is a lightness and naturalness about it akin to the later children's verse of Lewis Carroll and R. L. Stevenson.

Roscoe wrote religious verse, too, as might be expected of a serious-minded Nonconformist. In 1818 he edited the hymnal of the chapel he attended in Renshaw Street, composing many of the hymns. His poetry was the natural outflow of all his emotions and is interesting because it tells us so much about him.

It is hard to know in which order to unravel the many strands of Roscoe's varied interests and achievements. Each one is so intertwined with others. His poetry so frequently is woven in with his political activities as well as his philanthropy and promotion of culture. He had already attacked the slave trade in *Mount Pleasant*. In 1787 and 1788 he launched into the attack even more drastically with the poems *The Wrongs of Africa* and *The African* as well as in prose. The later poem was a joint effort with Dr James Currie a Scottish-born local doctor. The profits of both poems went to the National Committee for the Abolition of the Slave Trade. Roscoe and Currie had taken to each other naturally, both being interested in the arts and in bettering social conditions. Along with William Rathbone, the Quaker merchant, Edward Rushton, the blind but resourceful ex-mate of a slave ship, later a tavern keeper, editor and bookseller who wrote the *West Indian Eclogues*, a collection of anti-slave trade verse, certain Nonconformist ministers and other friends, they formed an informal literary and cultural club, with political reforming aims as an ulterior bond. They alike attacked the rotten boroughs and the corruption associated with the pre-1832 Parliament, the religious tests for public office and the trade monopoly of the East India Company. Hating all oppression, they supported the French Revolution, which broke out in 1789 and led to war with France.

Although Roscoe and his colleagues were a minority in Liverpool, they were part of a very widespread movement against the slave trade. The Society for the Abolition of Slavery was founded in 1787 with Thomas Clarkson as its secretary. William Pitt, the then Prime Minister, and Charles James Fox, his political opponent, were both united in opposition to the slave trade.

Clarkson visted Liverpool collecting data and exhibits. The slave traders tried to drown him in the Mersey!

Roscoe and his friends were indeed brave to champion so unpopular a cause in the Liverpool of 1787. The populace generally were against them from the beginning; the candidates for Parliament in 1790 threatened a dire economic fate for Liverpool and dire happenings—at the hands of the mob—for the anti-slave trade party if an abolition bill were passed in Parliament. From 1792 these mounting threats, combined with the unexpected progress of events in France, made the abolitionists feel that they had no alternative but to lie low for a while. Indeed, even their cultural meetings were suspended.

The situation was indeed complex. With all the variety of advanced causes which these men championed, they encountered opposition on every front at once. In their support of the French Revolution, advocacy of peace with France and agitation for the dismissal of Pitt, they ultimately did harm to the purely humanitarian causes which they favoured. The execution of Louis XVI in January 1793 seemed to Dr Currie 'a deliberate and dreadful murder'. Even Rathbone, a thorough Radical, realised that 'the business of reform in England was implicated with it and is become still more unpopular in these parts . . . we are therefore quiet'. Roscoe, as we might expect, had written poems in honour of the French Revolution, thinking it would correspond to England's 'Glorious Revolution' of 1688. One of these poems, set to music, became a popular 'hit'. He attacked the conservative views of Burke in a skit entitled *The Life, Death and Wonderful Atchievements of Edmund Burke*, which, though clever, was on a level with the street ballad. However, when, in the autumn of 1793, his French Revolution heroes, the Girondin deputies, were executed by the Jacobin faction, his political views must have become confused even in his own mind. It is hard to be a martyr when this is so, as he and his fellow-thinkers found. Hence Currie plunged into medical and social work among the poor, and later for the French prisoners of war. Rathbone, changing from Quaker to Unitarian, steeped himself in religious meditation. Roscoe's recourse was to his books, his manuscripts, his paintings and his plants.

It was in 1795 that he achieved fame for his Life of Lorenzo de Medici. He had been ruminating over the project for years, and undoubtedly saw himself as a latter day Lorenzo, leading a commercial community to cultural pre-eminence. His old friend, the banker, William Clarke, junior, lived near Florence on account of his health and collected material there for him. It seems unlikely that the work would have appeared so soon had not Roscoe suffered an enforced retirement from the political scene. It was the foremost work on the subject for over a generation. Of this work Horace Walpole said that 'he had not enjoyed such unexpected pleasure for a long time'. Some enthusiasts compared him with Gibbon. It was translated into French, German and Italian. It brought Roscoe on to the international horizon and went through many editions.

For some time, despite the regular increase of family responsibilities, the outlay of his public activities, as well as his good works, Roscoe had been prospering enough to collect works of art and to sponsor the arts in various ways. He founded a society for the encouragement of designing, drawing and painting in 1772, celebrating this by composing an ode. He arranged the first art exhibition ever held in Liverpool in 1774. Between 1780 and 1790 he collected prints. When the original art society failed, he founded another in 1784, which was in turn succeeded by 'The Academy for the Encouragement of the Fine Arts', at a meeting of which he gave a lecture entitled *The Progress and Vicissitudes of Taste*. From the collecting of prints, he graduated to drawings and then, as wealth increased, to original paintings. He corresponded with, patronized and largely kept together the body and soul of the hot-blooded, radical, witty, romantic-sensational painter Fuseli. Roscoe's collection of paintings consisted mainly of Italian 'Primitives', though there were some early Dutch and Flemish. The gem of the collection is the painting by Simone Martini in 1342 entitled 'Christ Returning from the Doctors to his Parents'.

Fine books, too, he collected, including early

The Gem of Roscoe's Art Collection: Christ discovered in the Temple by Simone Martini, painted for the Pope in 1342.

printed works such as Wynkyn de Worde's *Golden Legend*, and also valuable manuscripts.

In 1798, he, with Dr Currie and others established the Athenaeum, still a famous club and independent library in Liverpool. In 1813 he helped to found the Liverpool Royal Institution.

All kinds of sciences interested him. His first love was botany. In 1802 the first Botanic Garden in Liverpool was opened. Roscoe took a leading part in its establishment. He corresponded with Sir James Smith, F.R.S., President of the Linnaean Society. Roscoe himself cultivated exotic plants in his own garden and placed the choicest specimens in the Botanic Gardens' herbarium. Some of these still survive in the Merseyside County Museums. One particular group of plants fascinated him—the Scitaminaeae. These plants

49

yield certain well-known condiments, such as ginger. He read papers on them and finally in 1828, produced a luxurious illustrated work on the subject. It is now a collectors' item. He was then 75 years old.

In 1805 Roscoe's second work on Italian history came out, *The Life and Pontificate of Leo X*. Roscoe himself thought it better than his work on Lorenzo. It, too, was a considerable success amongst European readers. Leo was a member of the Medici family. It was he whose hard bargaining with German princes and bishops in order to raise funds for building St Peter's precipitated the actions of Martin Luther. British readers did not take so kindly to the admiration of such a pope.

Roscoe's Italian interests continued all his life. In 1822 he produced an edition, with a laudatory preface, of Alexander Pope, who, as a staunch Monarchist, was an odd choice for Roscoe to favour. This work involved Roscoe in some controversy. He planned many other projects, too, which never went into print.

Agriculture, too, was a hobby of Roscoe. In 1792 he joined a partnership to reclaim Chat Moss, a notorious wilderness just south of the town of Leigh. He did work of great value there and published a book in 1815 about his improvements.

He corresponded with many great agriculturists, including the famous 'Coke of Norfolk'. In 1814 he visited him at Holkham Hall. There Coke's uncle had amassed a vast library of classical manuscripts. Roscoe was in his element. He helped to catalogue them.

In view of all these activities he was elected a member of the Linnaean Society for his botany and a Royal Associate of the Royal Society of Literature for his writings. The latter honour carried a pension of £100 a year.

When, may we ask did this 'man of parts' find time to do a normal day's work? He was a practising lawyer. Till 1790 he lived in Liverpool town near his office. In 1790 he moved to Toxteth Park, then still in the 'green belt'. He there wrote a poem called *The Dingle*. Dingle Point then provided a fine view of Liverpool Bay—a thought for those that catch the bus from the Dingle today! Business, cultural and social interest drew him back in 1793 to Folly Lane, now Islington, till

Allerton Hall, Liverpool, one of Roscoe's homes.

1799. As a partner with the firm of Aspinall and Lace, leading lawyers for many commercial firms, he, like many lawyers, could hardly fail to prosper in a prospering town and port, albeit partly on account of the slave trade. In a rapidly expanding town, moreover, land values rose meteorically. Roscoe reaped the benefit of this too. It was an environment for making fortunes. His short-term banking partner, Thomas Leyland, and Sir John Gladstone, father of the famous statesman, were outstanding examples of this. But Roscoe, when his life of Lorenzo had brought him fame, yearned for retirement. Thus when Allerton Hall came on the market in 1799 he immediately bought it, in hopes of indulging further in writing and collecting.

Yet, sadly, even there business commitments caught up with him. The father of his friend William Clarke, junior, died. The London banker with whom Clarke and Sons were involved made investigations. He was impressed by Roscoe's handling of the matter as a lawyer and urged him to become a partner. In fact, he threatened to bring bankruptcy proceedings if Roscoe refused. Being satisfied that, when normal trading was resumed after the war, the bank could meet all demands, Roscoe became, in the year 1800, a banker. Yet it was during those years as a banker in spite of himself, that he achieved so much of cultural significance. More amazing still, he reached the highest point, even if somewhat of an anti-climax, of his public career.

The situation in France had changed. Under Napoleon it was virtually a monarchy. It was not now a question of revolutionary principles so much, but of how far Britain should go in seeking peace with France. The view of Fox was that the French Revolutionaries had been wrong in many ways, but that this was understandable and should be forgiven. Despite the defeat of his navy at Tralfalgar, Napoleon's armies were victorious when Pitt died in Jan. 1806. There was a wind of change blowing. Fox, now Roscoe's hero, was asked to form a ministry. It was a time for new voices to be heard. Why not a new voice from Liverpool, and that voice to be Roscoe's?

In 1806, then, just when his banking concerns were falling heavily upon him, Roscoe was asked to stand for Parliament, as a Whig, of course, sup-porting the abolition of the slave trade, peace with France and any reforming measures going. People were tired of the two retired generals who had represented Liverpool of late. Arthur Heywood, the banker, was now geared to organise the electioneering machine, having at his service clerks employed by the American merchant houses in Liverpool, whose masters were eager to press on with trade as of old, which the war was damaging. A young Liverpool merchant, already rapidly accumulating riches, sat on the election committee. His name was John Gladstone, whose son William was to be a power in Parliament for most of the century. Twelve thousand pounds was discreetly disbursed in the election on Roscoe's behalf.

It could have been Roscoe's finest hour. The times were in his favour. The Liverpool voters, convinced now that the slave trade would soon be abolished anyway, were prepared to support Roscoe. He, on his side, was prepared to advocate gradual abolition and plead for adequate compensation. He was also to press for the abolition of the trade monopoly of the East India Company. This, it was hoped, would provide an alternative trading sphere for Liverpool.

In Parliament, however, Roscoe failed to match his noble spirit with eloquent words. Maybe the gross place-seeking of many M.P.'s distressed him. He missed his family. His banking affairs troubled him. Having taken the rich slaving banker, Leyland, into partnership in 1802, to strengthen the concern, nevertheless he dissolved the partnership at the end of 1806. In the House he failed to say the right things about compensation on the slave trade issue and did not press the cause of the American merchants urgently enough. As expected, he supported every reforming measure, including Catholic Emancipation and Whitbread's bill for educating the poor, but failed to impress the House or constituents at home.

Parliament dissolved the next year. Roscoe realized that, as the abolition of the slave trade took effect, serious unemployment was arising. The East India Company's monopoly still held. He knew himself to be out of favour by the riots which greeted him on his return home. He declined to be re-nominated. Against his will, however, his name went forward, only to come bottom of the poll at the election. His friends were quick to tell him that the world was not worthy of him. He retired to his cultural pursuits.

The year 1815 brought the victory of Waterloo and peace at last. Roscoe was elected a freeman of the borough. But peace brought commercial tragedy to many, including Roscoe. He realized that trouble was brewing for those with financial entanglements. So, with characteristic nobility, he took the initiative to stave off disaster for all involved. His bank suspended payments, but he calculated that the assets of the partners would well cover all debts. But in those depressed times nothing sold for its expected value. In 1816 Roscoe sold his library and pictures. His friends rallied round and bought some of the best books and pictures intending to present them to him. He declined this, hence the books went to the Athenaeum Library and the pictures to the Royal Institution. Most of these came later to the Walker Art Gallery.

The landed estates of the partners including Allerton Hall, were put up for sale. They did not sell readily. In 1820 the partners were declared bankrupt. It is good to know, however, that, thanks to mining investments, the bankruptcy was annulled in 1843.

Roscoe went to live in Lodge Lane, then just outside the borough boundary. He continued his learned pursuits. In 1819 he produced a discourse on the treatment of criminals and was unwearied in putting forward his advanced views not only to his fellow-countrymen but to the rest of the world also. Likewise he continued to press for the abolition of slavery on an international scale. Three years before he died he helped to form an Association for Superseding the Use of Children in Sweeping Chimneys. He wrote a pamphlet in 1822 to raise money for the clothing of a Welsh vagrant with a remarkable gift for languages.

We have seen how Roscoe's mind continued active in the arts and sciences to the end. It must have given him great pleasure to meet and help Audubon, the great ornithological artist, who visited Liverpool in 1826. Audubon could hardly have paid him a greater compliment than he did when he named a bird *Roscoe's Yellow Throat*. From 1827 illness reduced his powers. Yet he still had

energy to write to La Fayette in 1830, urging him to use mercy following the arrests in France.

He died in 1831 aged 77. His name was later given to a chair of Architecture and Applied Art at the University of Liverpool. The garden of rest around his grave is the only preserved portion of Renshaw Street Unitarian Chapel yard, the yard of the chapel he attended, at the foot of Mount Pleasant.

The memorial, I think, he would himself have chosen is the beautiful group of flowers which grow 9,000 feet up in the Himalayas, the Roscoeas, named by Sir James Smith, founder and first president of the Linnaean Society in honour of his friend.

Derivative in his verse, unsuccessful in politics, ill fated in business, yet a perfect example of the cultured gentleman—and a friend to all in need and to every worthwhile cause, to quote the American writer Washington Irving: 'Where ever you go in Liverpool, you perceive traces of his footsteps in all that is elegant and liberal'.

Sir John Barrow: Patron of Exploration, 1764—1848

Portrait of Barrow as a young man.

In the district of Furness, on Hoad Hill, overlooking Ulverston and Morecambe Bay, stands a tower the shape of the old Eddystone Lighthouse. It is the Barrow Memorial, perpetuating the name of Sir John Barrow, who was born in 1764 in a cottage at Dragley Beck, a hamlet just outside Ulverston. As the children sang when the foundation stone of the tower was laid, he was:

> . . . the Town Bank scholar
> Who once was poor as we,
> And won his way by merit
> To wealth and high degree.

His name has no connection with the nearby town of Barrow-in-Furness, but his name is found the remotest corners of the world. For the northernmost cape of the American continent is called Point Barrow, while the strait leading west out of Lancaster Sound, near the North Magnetic Pole, is named Barrow Strait.

Barrow wrote up his life story at the age of eighty three. The cottage where he was born still stands. His father was only a smallholder and John was educated at the local grammar school. He refers to his time there as his happiest days. In addition to classical literature he learned the useful arts of casting accounts and surveying. At the age of thirteen he obtained his first job of assistant surveyor on a local estate. He also improved his mind in his own time. He founded a young astronomers' club. A few miles away lived a highly reputed amateur astronomer, Gibson, to whom Barrow constantly resorted with mathematical problems. He also made an electric kite, after the pattern of Benjamin Franklin, with which he gave an old lady a shock! He had an early interest in botany, tending the flower garden at home. He befriended a wounded midshipman, son of a local farmer. What he learned from him of navigation and the sea he found enthralling. The 'Middy' in turn learned classics from Barrow and entered the ministry. By chance Barrow heard of an opening as an apprentice accounts clerk at Walker's foundry, Liverpool. He left home to take the job when only fourteen. Before he had served his articles, however, his master died and he seized the opportunity to go on a whaling ship to Spitzbergen. He enjoyed his time at sea and secured some whale jawbones as a souvenir. He did not see himself as a seaman, though. On his return, he learned, through his astronomer friend Gibson, of a vacancy for a mathematics tutor at Greenwich Academy, a school for naval officers' sons. He went up to London and got the job.

The salary was not high, but Barrow did some private teaching too. He filled his spare time up with mind-improving activities still, having a confessed hatred of idleness. He impressed the eccentric colonial administrator, **Sir George Staunton**, with his abilities, particularly in astronomy, and was appointed tutor to Staunton's precocious son, who, at the age of twelve, spoke five languages including Chinese. Sir George was the friend and advisor of Lord McCartney, a leading 18th century diplomat who took an embassy to China in 1792.

Young Barrow went on this embassy as Comptroller of the Household. Sir George was deputy. Thus already, though only twenty eight, Barrow had, without University education or inherited wealth, established himself as an intelligent and reliable administrator and found, from now on, an effective patron in Lord McCartney.

Henceforth Barrow's life becomes intensely interesting. At a time when geographical knowledge was increasing, Barrow was in a favoured position. His fluent pen was to serve the cause of exploration, scientific discovery and naval history.

When in China, Barrow kept his eyes open and made interesting notes. In 1804 he published *Travels in China*, to supplement the official account. His supplement was more popular than the official version. When the party had landed in China, the long trek to Peking began. With the escort which the Emperor sent, the ambassador's party was swelled to a small army, with 3,000 porters, 85 wagons, 209 horses and 8 field guns. Barrow was responsible for the accommodation of the staff and the safety of the gifts for the Emperor. These included certain products of Western science, such as a 'planetarium', which the expedition's 'philosopher', a Dr Dinwiddie, was to demonstrate.

Accommodation was first provided at the disused and dilapidated summer palace just outside Peking. The embassy requested better quarters. A palace was provided in Peking which Barrow described as fit for pigs. He describes the palaces and gardens in some detail, but critically. The Emperor inspected the presents, but did not request Dinwiddie to perform. He accepted them, however, but, apart from the Wedgwood ware, he consigned it all to a lumber room.

Despite the Emperor's courteous reception, he had no desire to have intercourse with the Western world. Thus the embassy was unsuccessful. On the way back Barrow made a number of excursions and tried out his Chinese. He observed with distaste, that there was 'not a water-closet in all China'.

For Barrow the embassy had been worthwhile for the knowledge obtained. He summed up his view of the Chinese thus:

At the moment, compared with Europe, they (the Chinese) can only be said to be great in trifles, while they are really trifling in everything that is great . . .

Nevertheless he concluded that:

In our estimation of the character of the Chinese, on leaving England, we were far from doing them that justice which . . . we found them to deserve.

His conclusion was that the Chinese mind was first rate itself but 'confined . . . to one fixed . . . course through life, . . . no progressive improvement can therefore be looked for . . . no discovery in arts or science'.

McCartney's next summons was to Cape Colony as first governor, in 1797. The Cape, originally Dutch, was annexed when France overran Holland. Barrow was asked to go with McCartney as private secretary.

Barrow's inquiring mind jumped at the chance. The Dutch had done very little in the way of studying the country with a view to development.

The Admiralty Board Room in Barrow's time, c. 1810.

Their maps were inadequate. Barrow made a statistical survey, a census, and, in 1799 produced the first accurate map of the Colony. These were the fruit of his special assignment to settle the quarrels between the Boers and the Kaffirs. This involved a five hundred mile journey. Every day Barrow wrote up his observations and arranged his botanical specimens. He had an interview with the Kaffir king, with whose physique and good sense he was much impressed. He tried hard to cure the Boers of their inhumanity to the Bushmen and the Hottentots. For this good work his salary was doubled, whereupon Barrow married the daughter of a local judge.

Barrow's reports are good reading, with full descriptions of the natives. But for a personal slant on life in the Colony the letters of Lady Anne Barnard, the wife of the secretary of the Colony, should be read. She held endless parties which broke the ice between the Dutch and British effectively. She described Barrow as 'one of the pleasantest, best informed and most eager-minded young men in the world about everything curious or worth attention'. She and he went up Table Mountain together. They sang 'God Save the King' from the top.

In 1803 the Cape was returned to the Dutch. Barrow was sorry to leave. But it was retaken in

1806. Barrow saw its strategic importance and kept it before the Government, so that in the peace of 1815 it was retained. He was thus initially responsible for the Simonstown base, then called Simons Bay. His views on the racial problem were far in advance of his time. Barrow's book on his travels in Southern Africa, attractively illustrated by Daniell, was a great success.

The book attracted the attention of Lord Melville, who as Secretary for War and the Colonies, had been behind the move to seize the Cape. He and William Pitt, now out of office, invited Barrow to dine with them on his return. Melville persuaded Barrow to add a second volume stressing the strategic and commercial potential of South Africa. When Pitt came back to power the next year, Melville was made First Lord of the Admiralty and, on McCartney's recommendation, Barrow was appointed Second Secretary.

Barrow began his new job at a time of crisis. The peace of 1803 had been expected to last and the previous First Lord had let the Navy run down. Barrow was therefore involved in the frantic efforts to revive the Navy in time for Trafalgar. He was to remain Second Secretary from 1803 till 1845, retiring at the age of eight one, apart from a short intermission in 1806. The salary was £2,000 a year in war-time and £1,500 in peace-time. The most junior of the twenty six clerks in the Admiralty office earned £150 a year. Barrow saw his post develop into that of a permanent appointment, independent of political alignment. The Board Room at the Admiralty is now much as it was in Barrow's time. Barrow claimed to be the last man to see Nelson officially before he went down to Portsmouth; yet at the time of the Trafalgar campaign a great row was brewing at the Admiralty. Melville was accused of misappropriation of public funds and resigned. The shock of it may well have hastened Pitt's death. But Barrow was fully immersed in his administrative work in the hope of the victory which came at Trafalgar. His personal indebtedness to Melville, however, made him partisan and he was henceforth to be a life-long Tory.

With Pitt's death, the Whigs came into power and Barrow temporarily lost his job. Next year, however, the Tories were back again and so was Barrow, never to leave till retirement. All the evidence points to much hard work on the part of both Secretaries in making an outdated system work as best it could. Barrow's hatred of idleness stood him in good stead.

With the advent of peace, Barrow's active mind thought of work for the Navy to do.

To what purpose could a portion of our Naval force be more honourably or usefully employed than in completing those details of geographical and hydrographical science of which the grand outlines have been boldly and broadly sketched by Cook, Vancouver and Flinders?

Barrow wrote this in his introduction to Tuckey's account of his voyage to the Congo in 1816, for which Barrow had been responsible. In co-operation with Sir Joseph Banks, President of the Africa Association and of the Royal Society, and other scientists, Captain Tuckey was sent out to explore the Congo. The expedition is significant in that an attempt was made to use a 'steam sloop', H.M.S. Congo. She was the first steam ship built by the Navy. Since she could not go faster than 3 knots, it was decided to make her a schooner instead. The expedition was a disaster. Nearly all the men died including the scientists who went with the expedition. This was not surprising since tropical medicine was virtually unknown. The proceeds of the sales of Tuckey's journal went to help the widows and orphans.

Barrow wisely decided that the Arctic was a safer field. He had been on a whaler. Why not revive the ancient search for the North-West Passage? In 1818 Barrow published a book entitled *A Chronological History of Voyages into the Arctic Regions*. He expressed great optimism and a deep concern lest Russia should overtake Britain in this field.

The first expedition was not a success. Captain John Ross, the leader of the North-west Passage party, thought he saw a ring of mountains barring passage west from Baffin Bay. He turned back. The other party, which hoped to sail straight over the pole, was turned back by the ice. None of the other officers had seen the mountains reported by Ross. This gave rise to considerable feeling between Barrow and Ross, which never died down.

Ross's lieutenant, Parry, became Barrow's

favourite and made five voyages to the Arctic between 1818 and 1825.

The 1819/20 voyage effectively disproved the existence of Ross's mountains. Parry sailed on through Lancaster Sound and through what he then called Barrow Strait. When he reached 110° west, he announced to his crew that the £5,000 prize offered by the Government had been won. But after sailing past Melville Island (also so named by Parry) they reached the impenetrable ice of Beaufort Sea. Parry then put into a sheltered cove and prepared to winter in the ice in the hope that it might clear by the next summer. There they stayed from 26th Sept. 1819 till 1st Aug. 1820, the first explorers to spend a winter in the Arctic. The crews beguiled the long Arctic night with various entertainments including a comic newspaper. Canned vegetables and lime juice kept scurvy at bay. Summer came but the ice to the west still held. Nonetheless Parry returned to England convinced that he had proved the existence of the North-West Passage.

In his next expedition two winters were spent in the ice. His optimism never flagged. But it was not till 1903/4 that Amundsen succeeded in travelling through the elusive Passage. Parry's last voyage was an attempt to reach the North Pole from Spitzbergen, by dragging 'sledge boats' over the ice if necessary. The ice was far too rugged however, and the polar current worked against them constantly. Nonetheless Parry reached 84° 45′ N—a record for fifty years.

John Franklin went on two overland expeditions in Northern Canada, the objective being suggested by Barrow and the Admiralty providing the men. Barrow's plan was that Franklin would meet Parry's expedition on the coast. 600 miles of coast line were charted by Franklin and his men. But they never met Parry. On the return march they would have died of starvation had they not fed on a type of lichen. But adventure was in Franklin's blood and he made a similar expedition in 1825. Further valuable survey work was done then as well. Later expeditions were sponsored by the Royal Geographical Society, founded by Barrow.

It was not till 1844 that the Admiralty was willing to send another expedition to seek the cherished North-West Passage. The time seemed favourable. The steam ships 'Erebus' and 'Terror', fresh from the Antarctic, were ready for use. Other naval powers were threatening to rival Britain. Franklin, though now 59, was keen to press forward again. Barrow, now over 80, drew up the instructions. The expedition took food for three years. This was why, when Barrow died in 1848, he was still hopeful of good news. He never knew that in fact one of the greatest tragedies in the history of Arctic exploration had occurred.

Barrow's general enthusiasm for science has already been mentioned. In 1806, as a friend of Sir Joseph Banks, the 'grand old man' of science, he was elected F.R.S., mainly for his botanical work in China and South Africa. He was elected to the council in 1815. At the time of his death he was working on *Sketches of the Royal Society and the Royal Society Club*. He found a kindred spirit in the great Henry Cavendish, who likewise had north Lancashire connections.

The Royal Geographical Society developed from a club devoted to travellers' tales. The idea of a Geographical Society was in the air and Barrow chaired a meeting at which the proposal to form the society was put. It was Barrow through whom royal patronage was obtained. He wrote the first article in the Society's Journal, and was president from 1835–37. The Admiralty and the Foreign Office worked closely with the Society in promoting exploration.

This first article was on the Swan River Colony in Western Australia. Barrow envisaged also a trading base near the modern Darwin, as a 'second Singapore'. Today it seems strategically an extremely good idea.

Barrow had a good flow of words. He was a regular writer for John Murray's *Quarterly Review*, a Tory magazine. Through Barrow, other explorer-writers were introduced to Murray. He wrote articles on naval matters for the Encyclopaedia Britannica. He also wrote popular lives of Peter the Great of Russia, Admirals Howe and Anson and an account of the Mutiny on the Bounty, which last work became a minor classic. Retiring at the age of 80, he wrote a sequel to his earlier work on Arctic voyages, taking his account to 1846. He also wrote his autobiography. He was writing the day before he died. His works are extremely readable and, for their time and pop-

PROCESSION UP HOAD-HILL, THE SITE OF THE MEMORIAL.

The procession at the founding of the monument to Sir John Barrow, 1850.

ular purpose, good and useful.

In 1835 Barrow became a baronet. During the year 1827–8, when the office of Lord High Admiral was revived for the Duke of Clarence, later William IV, Barrow was one of the few who got on well with the awkward and autocratic Duke. When the Duke became King and Sir Robert Peel was Prime Minister, the First Secretary to the Admiralty, Peel's friend, recommended Barrow to the honour of a baronetcy. Barrow hesitated at first, but finally yielded to friends' persuasion. The award was for 'eminence in science and literature'.

The reviewer of his autobiography summed him up thus: 'a sheet-anchor of Arctic exploration and obliging official to all'. Sir James Graham, twice First Sea Lord, described him as 'a public servant of the greatest merit, knowledge and experience'.

He was one of the greatest men of the Furness district of Lancashire. On his 80th birthday the rowan tree he planted as a boy was covered with flags and his health was drunk by the local people. Having helped to establish a Sunday School in Ulverston in his youth, in his will he left money for educational and charitable uses in his home district. There, though he is buried in London, his memory is perpetuated not only by Barrow Tower but by the benefits which the people with whom he always acknowledged the strongest bond, still enjoy.

Captain Crow—The Last Liverpool Slave Captain, 1765–1829

Liverpool breeds sailors. Their adventures have provided matter for best-selling novels. But one of these sea-dogs, Captain Hugh Crow, was able to write up detailed memoirs before he died. These writings give us a direct insight into the daily life of the typical merchant seaman, not only in his outward actions but in his inward feelings. Even if we make allowance for the gilding of early recollections written up in retirement, we are still left with a most enthralling residue.

For most of his career Crow was engaged in the slave trade—a despicable occupation, we might say. Yet, in an age as rough and tough as the 18th century, in which Crow was born, it must have been quite easy to regard it as not unduly cruel but merely a necessary evil. The discipline of seamen in the Royal Navy, or of soldiers in the army was ruthless and accepted as such. In an age that knew not anaesthetics, physical pain was not regarded as an avoidable evil. Crow's memoirs, however, reveal that despite his hard schooling at sea and his engaging in the slave trade, he had still a compassionate and kindly heart, a sense of values, as well as the professionally necessary qualities of resolution, courage, daring, endurance, aptitude for hard work and keen observation. He also had the knack of telling a good tale.

Like many fine sailors, he was born a Manxman and loved to fly the Three Legs of Man from the mast of his ship, to the amusement of the African populace. He lost an eye in childhood. At the age of seventeen he went on his first voyage, to the Barbadoes. The first leg was hard going—storms in the Irish Sea, sea-sickness and a leaky ship. His malady earned him the derision of older sailors. He was kept constantly at the pumps. A tough start to a tough life.

Captain Crow, late in life.

59

He early witnessed the cruelty of the press gang and the desperate endeavours the men made to escape, knowing the hard life of the Royal Navy. However, he loved the sea. He enjoyed the passage from Ireland to the West Indies. Having overcome his sea-sickness, his knowledge of nautical matters—he had yearned for the seafaring life from boyhood—came in useful and he was able to hold his own with the experienced sailors. For the voyage back he was made ship's carpenter, the previous one having deserted.

Fever, constant labour at the pumps, extremities of thirst and hunger, severe exposure, narrow escapes were his lot in his early voyages. He recalled chewing lead to stave off the pangs of thirst and fighting for his life when a fellow apprentice-sailor nearly threw him off the main-top. Despite all, he developed from his early years a strong sense of duty, a hatred of intemperance, extravagance and profligacy, and also a revulsion against all needless severity, such as the work of the press gang and the floggings in the army and the navy. He showed an active compassion and practical generosity to all in need. He could also laugh at his misfortunes and be magnanimous towards those who had wronged him. Above all, his trust in the mercy and providence of God rarely faltered. How he combined these qualities with employment in the slave trade we shall see later. It was in 1788 that he first became firmly associated with Liverpool commerce. The port of Liverpool was to hold his loyalty for the rest of his life. At first he would not touch the Africa or Guinea trade, as the slave trade was frequently called. 'I had an abhorrence of the very name of slave' he wrote. His mind was changed in the course of the next voyage.

In the summer of 1790 war seemed imminent. As his vessel came into the Mersey estuary, most of the men, and he with them, took to the boats to avoid the press gang. They were lucky to escape. His friends continued to urge on him the advantages of the Africa trade. Quietening his conscience with the reflection that the impressed seamen of England were virtually 'white slaves', as he put it, and could well be worse off than black slaves, he set sail in 'a beautiful brig' as chief mate, for the Gold Coast, now Ghana.

It is from this point on that Crow's fascinating observations of life at Bonny, Calabar and other parts of West Africa begin. He reported every item of interest that came to his knowledge. He spared no pains to understand, befriend and help the natives. He tried also to wean them from their cruel practices. On this, his first voyage, for instance, on the death of the local 'king', twenty three of the deceased ruler's wives were put to death!

On his next voyage he met a native pilot called 'My Lord', whose work was to propitiate the sharks, who were regarded as sacred, with offerings of brandy, beef and bread, in order that the ship might pass safely. On arrival, Crow saw a native play, with animals masks, the ingenuity of which he admired, but he deplored the prevalence of gambling among the natives. 'They reminded me of some of your young bloods at home', he remarked. He witnessed a trial by ordeal conducted by the Jew-Jew men. The suspect swam across a shark-infested creek. Mercifully surviving, he was regarded as proved innocent. The sacred sharks, regularly fed and protected by the priests, had at least this use! Crow remarked with favour on the co-operation of even the black 'cargo' in emergency, such as the need to right the ship when grounded, and related how, when a negro fell overboard while washing the decks, he himself took the boat out, leaky though it was, and searched for some time in a rough sea, with darkness falling, rescuing him in the nick of time. Such compassion marks Crow out from among his fellow slave captains and naturally earned him great popularity. When the slaves were finally sold at Dominica, the ship filled up with invalid soldiers and their wives. It was more difficult, Crow noted, to maintain order amongst them than amongst the negroes!

Crow was setting out as chief mate of the *Gregson* for the Cape Coast in June 1794, when, just off Guernsey, a well-armed and heavily manned French ship captured his ship and its crew. Crow gives us a first class account of his experiences as a prisoner of war in France. He recorded how he saw French people 'dragged to the guillotine like sheep to the slaughter'. 'One Sunday in particular I . . . saw one hundred and fifty fine looking women, who had been caught with a priest at prayers in a field, brutally driven into the town, where, without even the mockery of a trial, they were handed over to the public executioner'. He described the foul bread, maggoty soup, filth, vermin, disease, near-starvation and total disorder of the prisons in sickening detail, lightened only by the fortunate circumstance of the capture, en route from Lisbon, of Lady Fitzroy and her brother, the Hon. Henry Wellesley, the Duke of Wellington's brother and sister, who, having fortunately escaped being plundered, were able to alleviate the lot of many prisoners. After nearly five months imprisonment, when two thousand prisoners had died, they were marched away to other quarters and Crow himself fell ill in February 1795. Things seemed to have improved a little, for he, with others, went to a hospital, where bleeding 'in the upper parts of my feet' wrought a speedy recovery. In hospital, one of his fellow-officers gave him useful instruction in arithmetic and navigation by logarithms. Feeling better generally, he managed to escape.

After some narrow escapes he reached Le Havre where a Danish captain gave him a passage to England, and thus he returned to Liverpool.

On his next voyage a young sailor, giving the name of Jack Roberts, came aboard. 'He' drank grog, sang, chewed tobacco and seemed just like any other seaman. But soon it was discovered that 'Jack' was in fact called Jane. She was landed thereupon 'with all possible gentleness and soon afterwards married a respectable young man'.

Every voyage brought fresh experiences, including greater intimacy with the African chiefs. The voyage in the *James*, to the Bonny district, the last he made as mate, was most unusual. Having taken a cargo of negroes, the ship grounded and sprang a leak. Despite the combined efforts of whites and blacks, she became stranded in Bonny Creek. Thereupon the natives, regarding the ship as a lawful prize, began to plunder her. Crow was ready to defend his possessions by force, However, the two joint kings, Pepple and Holiday, with whom Crow was to develop very good relations, persuaded the people to stop. Crow had made himself ill with his efforts. On his recovery, the kings and their grandees invited him to enjoy his time of recuperation with them. At the Council Chamber of the primitive kingdom, called the 'Palaver House' (hence our word 'palaver') great sacrifices were offered to the accompaniment of music. He was told not to laugh or smile during the ceremony. This and the subsequent revelry, he learned, were a thank-offering to their god for casting up his ship on shore! Although he had lost his ship he soon got a passage back.

In 1798 Crow at last, at the age of thirty four, became master of a vessel, the *Will*. As captain, he was in a position to take full credit for the outcome of a voyage and to do all he could for the comfort of crew and cargo alike. On this voyage he erected a thatched house on deck 'for the accommodation and comfort of the slaves'.

The voyage of 1799–1800 involved two actions with French vessels, again both successful ones. In the first encounter, off the African coast, little damage was sustained. The second encounter, near Tobago, was a narrow escape. There were serious injuries, some fatal, to blacks and whites and much damage to the ship. On his arrival home, Crow was presented with a handsome silver tray by the Merchants and Underwriters of Liverpool for his bravery in his first encounter with the French vessels. The Underwriters of Lloyds Coffee House added to this a silver cup with a sum of money for his exertions in the encounter off Tobago. The cup itself was worth two hundred pounds.

Crow had already seen how the natives of Bonny practised human sacrifice. On another voyage he witnessed the sacrifice of a teenage girl to the sharks as an offering to the god of the north wind. Later, a chief of a hostile tribe was captured. A great feast was held, the captured chief being the principal dish! Crow again tried to convert his African friends as on many other occasions, but in vain. He records that the diners openly boasted of their delicious meal! These experiences confirmed him in his belief that the condition of Africans in slavery was no worse, and probably better, than their native state.

On his voyage back, in 1804, he had his narrowest escape from sinking while master of a ship. The gale lasted ten or twelve days. Waves carried away rails, stanchions and bulwarks, One wave went as high as the maintop and the mast was dashed to pieces. At one time the main deck

The 'Mary' fighting English Frigates, 1806.

was 'breast-high with water'. Even in those straits, he recalled the 107th psalm. His courage is magnified further when we read that his leg ulcer was still active and that, on arriving home, amputation was suggested. With the typical remark that he and his leg were 'too warm friends ever to part', he settled to a year of convalescence.

Fit again, he was soon back at sea. His worst seafight was yet to come. He was never nonplussed at the prospect, but kept his ship and crew constantly trained at the guns. Indeed, he encouraged the negroes by arranging shooting matches for them, with appropriate prizes of drink and smart clothing. In 1806, the year of the Berlin Decrees, by which Napoleon hoped to kill English trade, Crow had a suspicion trouble was near.

Sure enough, on 1st December, 1806, near Tobago, two powerful warships bore down on Crow's ship, the *Mary*. The *Mary* was ordered to bring to, in English. Crow knew this to be a frequent French trick and refused. Although night had fallen battled was joined. Though sandwiched between two attacking vessels Crow and his men fought with spirit. Action continued till morning, with injuries and death, to crew and cargo. In the early dawn, the Captain himself received a blow which knocked him unconscious. Assuming he was killed, both officers and men lost heart completely. Crow's courage was nearly inexhaustible and infectious. As he came to, he heard the words of his chief mate: 'Sir, we have struck the colours!' The thought of the disgrace of surrender overcame the Captain's pain, he raised himself up and urged them to fire three or four more shots, but in vain.

All was now prepared for surrender. As the boarding party mounted the gangway, it was observed that they were Englishmen! The *Mary* had been fighting English ships all along! Crow was in a frenzy of chagrin but the English officers of the warships were most understanding and sympathetic, realising that he could hardly be held to blame. They themselves had though that the *Mary* was a French Privateer.

Crow's popularity with crew and negroes was undiminished by these events. The slaves were generally in fine fettle and sold well. It is worth noting that every care was given to both black and white victims of the battle. The commander of one of the warships wrote out a certificate for Crow, exonerating him completely. Crow heard interesting news when he got to Kingston. A Liverpool ship had recently been captured by a French ship, using the simple device of hailing in English and showing English colours! Fortunately she was recaptured soon after. An interesting evidence was provided of Crow's popularity with the negroes. One Sunday, at Kingston, while Crow was still in his 'cot', no doubt recuperating, a crowd of black folk, all in Sunday best came to greet him. He greeted them as old friends and distributed money to them. They even composed a calypso in his honour. Crow still would have to face the ship-owners on his return. Fortunately the ship could be refitted and the *Mary* reached Liverpool to find that the slave trade had been abolished just the day before.

Crow had one more voyage. The *Kitty's Amelia* had already been cleared out before the Bill had passed. Crow took command of her. So he was able to say goodbye to his friends at Bonny. He had treated his black friends kindly, sought to help them in sickness and to give them some of the benefits of European civilisation. He made his last visit to the Palaver House. It was doubly sad because King Holiday's wife was dying of smallpox and the occasion was to debate what should be done. King Pepple opened proceedings in pidgin English. Crow smiled a little, involuntarily. He had not expected this. But Pepple noticed Crow's smile and burst into hearty laughter. Whereupon Crow, Pepple and others left the company in haste. Crow managed at length to sober Pepple down. He felt embarrassed, in view of Holiday's great distress for his Queen, that he had been the cause of unseemly behaviour on the part of Holiday's fellow-monarch.

The 'middle passage' from Africa to Jamaica was marred by an outbreak of violent illness caused by inadequate cleansing before the ship set out. Crow takes the occasion to explain how he fed and cared for his black cargo so as to minimise the risk of disease. He says:

We frequently bought from natives considerable quantities of dried shrimps to make broth; and a very excellent dish they made when mixed with flour and palm oil, and seasoned with pepper and salt. Both whites and blacks were fond of this mess. In addition to yams we gave them, for a change, fine shelled beans and rice cooked together, and this was served up to each individual with a plentiful proportion of the soup. On other days their soup was mixed with peeled yams cut up thin and boiled with a proportion of pounded biscuit. For the sick we provided strong soups and middle messes, prepared from mutton, goats' flesh, fowls, etc., to which were added sago and lilipees, the whole mixed with port wine and sugar. I am thus particular in describing the ingredients which composed the food of the blacks, to show that no attention to their health was spared in this respect. Their personal comfort was also carefully studied. On their coming on deck about eight o'clock in the morning, water was provided to wash their hands and faces, a mixture of lime juice to cleanse their mouths, towels to wipe with, and chew sticks to clean their teeth. A dram of brandy bitters was given to each of the men, and, clean spoons being served out, they breakfasted about nine o'clock. About eleven, if the day were fine, they washed their bodies all over. and after wiping themselves dry were allowed to use palm oil, their favourite cosmetic. Pipes and tobacco were then supplied to the men, and beads and other articles were distributed amongst the women to amuse them, after which they were permitted to dance and run about on deck to keep them in good spirits. A middle mess of bread and cocoanuts (sic) was given them about mid-day. The third meal was served out about three o'clock, and after everything was cleaned out and arranged below, for their accommodation, they were generally sent down about four or five in the evening.

63

Despite the disease, he reports that his cargo sold well. He was again greeted heartily by his old black friends, sometimes shaking hands all round 'a hundred times in an hour'. After a near-fatal bout of fever, Crow returned to Liverpool in August 1808, to captain a ship no more.

His heart had been in the Africa trade. Nonetheless, he tried hard but vainly to disuade his only son from a nautical career. He certainly took a pride in caring for both his crew and his cargo to an exemplary degree. He complimented Wilberforce to this extent regarding the legislation of 1792:

There were in 1792 many laws made for the better regulation of the African trade, of which every person acquainted with the business heartily approved. One of these enacted that only five blacks should be carried for every three tons burthen; and as Mr Wilberforce was one of the promoters of these very proper regulations, I take this opportunity of complimenting him for the first and last time . . . Not a word was said about the white slaves, the poor sailors; these might die without regret. . . , In the African trade, as in all others, there were individuals bad as well as good, and it is but justice to discriminate, and not condemn the whole for the delinquencies of a few.

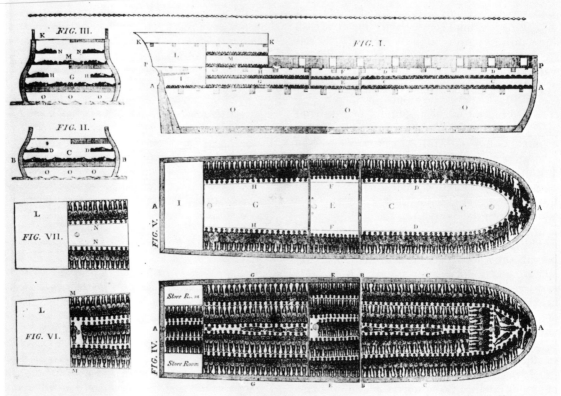

DESCRIPTION OF A SLAVE SHIP.

Slave packing, 1789.

His considered views he expressed thus:

The abolition was a severe blow for England, and particularly as it affected the interests of the white slaves who found employment in the trade. It has always been my decided opinion that the traffic in negroes is permitted by that Providence that rules over all, as a necessary evil. . . . One thing is clear: instead of saving any of the poor Africans from slavery, these pretended philanthropists, have, through the abolition, been the (I admit indirect) cause of the death of thousands: for they have caused the trade to be transferred to other nations, who, in defiance of all that our cruisers can do to prevent them, carry it on with a cruelty to the slaves, and a disregard of their comfort and even of their lives, to which Englishmen could never bring themselves to resort. . . . I owe it to myself, here to disclaim being a friend to slavery. God forbid that I should favour a system through which my fellow creatures should suffer any species of oppression, hardship, or injustice! I consider that the abolitionists have not understood the subject, and that their measures have done nothing towards the real abatement of slave-dealing in Africa,

I would rather be a black slave in the West Indies, than a white one at home . . . . Think of the miserable beings employed in our coal-pits. . . . Think of all the men, women, and children, confined by hundreds, in heated factories, their health rapidly wasting, and their earnings scarce sufficient to keep soul and body together.

His point is clear. After retiring from the sea, he tried life as a small farmer back in his native isle. But he could not be long away from Liverpool and his fellow sea-dogs, who met at the Lyceum newsroom. He died in his 64th year and is buried in Maughold churchyard, near his parents for whom he had provided most generously.

We can rightly say he was mistaken and misguided. But we have then said all that can be said against him. In respect of courage and compassion, combined with a sparkling sense of humour and supported by a firm faith in God and a strong sense of duty, Captain Hugh Crow may indeed have a few equals, but none that excel him.

Elizabeth Gaskell, Author and Housewife, 1810—1865

Mention Mrs Gaskell and everybody thinks of *Cranford*. But, to parody Kipling, one may well say: 'What should they know of Elizabeth Gaskell who only the writer of Cranford know?' For she was also a dutiful housewife, affectionate mother, energetic traveller, keen observer, a minister's wife, a person of deep sensitivity and compassion.

Her life coincided with an era of immense and traumatic changes. The landed classes were losing their hereditary position, while the people were losing those to whom they had from time immemorial looked for protection. Those that gravitated into the industrial towns found themselves under a factory master. Some of these were a kind of industrial squire, like Arkwright, but most were hard-headed, seeing all in terms of profit and loss, supply and demand, with no time for or sense of human values and without any tradition of public duty. Fluctuations of trade might bring 'laying off' and wage cuts to the hands, or even bankruptcy to the master. Railways, beginning with the Liverpool & Manchester, opened in 1830, were to bring town and country closer together in the north west and the north west closer to the rest of the country. Beginning with the reform of Parliament in 1832, everything else was reformed in due course, Corporations, Poor Relief, Public Health, education, mines and factories. Commissions sat and produced horrifying revelations. Working men agitated for the People's Charter. In the city of Manchester a German merchant, Engels, was compiling *The Condition of the Working Class in England*, published 1844, which exposed the seamy side of Britain's prosperity and led to the Communism of Marx. In 1842 the average life expectation of a Manchester factory worker was 17 years.

Mrs Elizabeth Gaskell.

To this world Elizabeth Stevenson came when she married William Gaskell, the junior minister of Cross Street Unitarian Chapel, Manchester. But she was born in London, where her father was Keeper of the Treasury Records. He had himself once been a Unitarian minister near Manchester. Through an earlier minister of Cross Street Chapel he had met his wife, a Holland, of Sandlebridge near Knutsford, a member of a family descended from ancient Lancashire stock. Elizabeth's father was a most versatile man. He had taught classics, edited a magazine, and dabbled in scientific farming! Elizabeth's mother died when the child was a year old. She was sent to Knutsford to be cared for by her maternal aunt. Knutsford became her 'dear, adopted native town', and still remains much as she knew it. Yet Knutsford is only 16 miles from Manchester, which became the Drumble of *Cranford*, and was soon to be linked to it by the 'nasty railroad'. In her aunt's household, also Unitarian, Elizabeth was schooled in piety, duty and honour, manners, modesty in dress and domestic economy. About 1822 she went to school in Stratford on Avon. Here she absorbed the beauty of the Warwickshire countryside and observed the ways of a society rooted in the past which she reflected in *My Lady Ludlow*. The schoolmistress was Anglican; Elizabeth attended Shakespeare's church and came to love the Prayer Book and English Church architecture. She was also in a literary atmosphere and it is noteworthy that her earliest published work was probably a school exercise, written after a visit to Clopton House near Stratford.

When her father became ill she spent much time with him. She was his only surviving child by his first marriage, for her brother John, like Peter Jenkyns in *Cranford*, sailed to India and never returned. For further experience of London life, she stayed with her Uncle, Swinton Holland, in Park Lane. Her cousin, Sir Henry Holland, became Physician to Prince Albert. Her knowledge of London life, to the shallowness of which she was clearly sensitive, provided material for parts of *North and South*. Sir Henry had been a pupil of the Rev. William Turner of Newcastle-on-Tyne, another Unitarian Minister of considerable culture. Elizabeth became friends with

his daughter and during the great cholera epidemic of 1831 they both spent some time in Edinburgh. There Elizabeth had her portrait painted and a bust executed. Towards the end of 1831, the two girls visited another daughter of Mr Turner, who was the wife of the Minister of Cross Street Chapel, Manchester. Thus, the wheel turned full circle and young Elizabeth found herself at the place where her father had made the contact that led to his marriage. Here she met William Gaskell, of an ancient Lancashire Presbyterian family, then Junior Minister at Cross Street. He, too, was highly accomplished. He was to become senior Minister in 1854 and to be Professor of English History and Literature at Manchester New College, the Unitarian Seminary. He also gave many lectures to working men and engaged in much public work. Even the loyal Anglican Winkworth sisters admitted that no Anglican they knew had the 'commanding intellect' of Gaskell as a teacher or preacher.

After an engagement of less than a year, they married in August 1832 at Knutsford Parish Church. According to custom, red and white sand was scattered in front of the houses, while the townsfolk sang to the newlyweds:

Long may they live,
Happy may they be.
And blest with a numerous
Pro-gen-y.

They had a beautiful honeymoon in North Wales. By September they were installed at Dover Street, Manchester, complete with a Broadwood Piano costing £55.

Manchester—a 'City sacred to mammon'—was also a centre of Liberal political thought and of science and culture. Foul though it was, much of what is now suburban sprawl was then green fields, and Greenheys Field in Moss Side, where *Mary Barton* opens, was a convenient picnic spot for the operatives. Elizabeth's initial reactions to her new setting are mirrored in *North and South*. Initial revulsion was counterbalanced by absorption with the needs and feelings of the impoverished, work-worn, often sickly factory hands. Two daughters, Marianne in 1834 and Margaret Emily in 1837, were born to them. In 1837, too, she wrote *Sketches among the Poor* for

Blackwood's Magazine. In 1838 she described a visit to Rivington and a walk up the Pike, in the first of many letters about visits to the more beautiful parts of Lancashire. 'Such a very pretty place and so thoroughly country,' she wrote. 'Yesterday morning I sketched . . . Rivington air has done wonders'. Another letter of 1838 is a mine of information on local folklore, including a ghost story about the old Lord Willoughby at Rivington. In 1841 she toured the Rhineland. In 1844 her son William was born, only to die before his 1st birthday. The first novel, *Mary Barton*, sprang from this tragedy, as an occupational therapy. She was to have two more daughters after this.

Charming stories for *Howitt's Journal*, although her tale *The Sexton's Hero* has pathos in its dramatic description of a traveller caught by the tide while crossing Morecambe Sands, did not involve her personality deeply enough to lift her mind from her grief. She loved the country best, yet somehow, as she admits in her introduction, she was most stirred by the thought of 'how deep might be the romance in the lives of those who elbowed me in the busy streets'. *Fraser's Magazine* asked: 'Do they want to know why poor men . . . learn to hate law and order, Queens, Lords and Commons, country-party and corn-law league alike—to hate the rich, in short? Then let them read *Mary Barton*. Do they want to know what can madden brave, honest, industrious north-country hearts, into self-imposed suicidal strikes, into conspiracy, vitriol-throwing and midnight murder? Then let them read *Mary Barton*'. She spoke of her novel as growing in her mind 'as imperceptibly as a seed germinates in the earth', her way to 'give utterance to the agony . . . of dumb people'. John Barton, whose daughter Mary gives the novel its title, is a radical, a Chartist. As he suffers and sees others suffering he becomes embittered. 'If I am out of work for weeks in bad times and winter comes . . . and there is no coal for the grate and no clothes for the bed, and the thin bones are seen through the ragged clothes, does the rich man share his plenty with me? . . . We're their slaves so long as we can work . . . and yet we are to live as separate as if we were in two worlds'. A petition to Parliament regarding the workers' grievances is a failure. A strike ensues. So incensed are the men by the contempt with which Harry Carson, the son of one of the masters, treats them, that a ballot is drawn for his murder. The lot falls to John Barton. Now Harry has been making advances to Mary, while she has scorned her true lover, Jem Wilson. As it happens John Barton borrows Jem's gun to commit the murder. The gun is found near the scene and Jem is charged. He is proved innocent by an alibi, obtained from a sailor-witness, who is brought back from his ship when just about to sail over the Mersey Bar. The dramatic race to catch the ship in time is an outstanding piece of writing. Meanwhile, John Barton, hounded by his conscience, confesses his guilt to the victim's father and finally expires in his arms. Mr Carson, who had hitherto thought only of vengeance, is impelled to repeat the text 'Forgive us our trespasses as we forgive them who trespass against us'.

Many descriptions are outstanding. Those of a cellar dweller who had been brought up in the dales of North Lancashire and still can make clap-bread, of the family from the country barely existing on 'Parish pay' and of the fire at Carson's Mill are haunting.

The theme is reconciliation. The bereaved father of the victim and the murderer, whose own son had died through malnutrition, meet as sharers of common sorrows. Job Legh, the non-political insect-collecting retired spinner, observes to Mr Carson: 'I never see the masters getting thin and haggard for want of food . . . it's in the things for show they cut short . . . what we all feel sharpest is the want of inclination to try and help the evils . . . if we saw our masters try . . . we'd bear up like men'. The authoress concludes: 'Many of the improvements now in practice in the system of employment in Manchester owe their origin to the short earnest sentences spoken by Mr Carson.'

The novel was an instant success. The Conservative Press generally accused Mrs Gaskell of radicalism and of an unequivocal embracing of the workers' cause. In fact, she tried to balance the viewpoints of both sides, but naturally, since the workers were the real sufferers, they had the stronger claim on her gift of pathos. But those that praised the work included Jowett, Master of Balliol College, Oxford; the Christian socialists,

The Drawing Room in Plymouth Grove, Manchester.

Kingsley and Maurice; Ruskin, Mrs Browning, Lord Shaftesbury, Dickens, Carlyle, and the aged Maria Edgeworth. Carlyle wrote: 'A book above the ordinary garbage of novels. May you long live to write good books'.

Social novels had been attempted before, but none with such sympathy and identity. Mrs Gaskell's crowning honour was an invitation to one of the literary breakfasts given by Samuel Rodgers, the London banker, in May 1849. She had already dined with Dickens and Carlyle in March.

Mrs Gaskell's head was brimfull of ideas for stories. Her letters reveal her active mind. Ever written in haste, in contrast to the slow, well-thought-out epistles of her husband, they leave the reader breathless. She wrote regularly for Dickens' Magazine, *Household Words*, much of it hackwork, for Dickens needed regular rather than brilliant contributions. Between 1851 and 1853,

Cranford came out in this Magazine. A greater contrast to her previous major work could hardly be conceived. *Cranford* dwells on the charms of the old-world life of Knutsford, which Mrs Gaskell had so loved, with its settled customs and standards. Yet this contrast was deep-rooted in Mrs Gaskell's personality. *Cranford* was a gem of its kind and gave scope for fine writing but it did not provide an outlet for her deepest self. When, in 1850, she was about to move to a better house in Plymouth Grove, in a letter she wondered whether:

'It is right to spend so much on so purely selfish a thing as a house is, while so many are wanting—that's the haunting thought to me; at least to one of my 'mes': for I have a great number and that's the plague. One of my 'mes' is, I do believe, a true Christian (only people call her socialist and communist) another of my 'mes' is a wife and mother, and highly delighted at the delight of everyone

69

else in the house . . . my 'social' self . . . another self with a full taste for beauty and convenience.'

Mrs Gaskell thus did not live wholly for literature. The other aspects of her life found expression *through* her literature. 'A good writer of fiction', she wrote 'must have lived an active and sympathetic life . . . When you are forty . . . you will write ten times as good a novel as you could do now, just because you will have gone through much more of the interests of a wife and a mother'.

Her sympathies found expression in her next novel *Ruth*, written in 1853, which dealt with the lot of the unmarried mother. An innocent young orphan girl, charmed by an irresponsible young gentleman, but deserted by him in the hour of need, is taken in by a Dissenting Minister. He and his sister—he is a bachelor— pretend she is a young widow. The Dissenting Chapel's leading layman, a rich merchant, engages her as a governess. Years pass, the illegitimate son grows up. The merchant sponsors an M.P. who is none other than the gentleman who got Ruth into trouble. He recognises Ruth and offers to marry her. She refuses, dramatically, nobly, and finally. There is an ironic picture of the pre-election discussions, in which the rather selfrighteous merchant is talked into condoning the bribery regarded as necessary by the candidate's agent. The Minister observes that we are not to practise evil that good may come, forgetting that he has lied to protect Ruth! Meanwhile, Ruth's secret gets to the merchant's ears. Outraged, he dismisses her and dissociates himself from the Minister and the Chapel. A cholera outbreak occurs. Ruth alone volunteers to nurse the victims. One of her patients is the M.P. who caused her fall. From him she catches the infection and dies. Thus she pays her debt to society. The proud merchant, humbled by this, and by a family disgrace, returns to the Chapel, a sadder and wiser man. The local Doctor adopts Ruth's son.

A storm broke around Mrs Gaskell's ears. She was shunned in her husband's own Chapel. She was accused of having allowed 'a demoralising laxity to go unchecked'. However, *North British Review* commented favourably. Charlotte Bronte wrote warmly: 'Nor have you ever excelled the power of certain passages'. Mrs Gaskell did much work for 'fallen women'. She had practical experience on which to draw.

Over her next novel *North and South* she quarrelled with Dickens. The problems was that a novel does not always lend itself to serial treatment. She herself regarded it as her favourite work. Set, like *Mary Barton*, in 'dear old ugly, smoky, grim, grey Manchester', we have already seen how it reflects the writer's experience. But in this work she tried to bring out much more of the viewpoint of the manufacturer. Her husband's cousin, Holbrook Gaskell, was a partner with Nasmyth in his great engineering works near Eccles. No doubt she drew on what she had heard him and his fellow industrialists say. In the novel, *Thornton*, the manufacturer, speaking of the development of machinery, says:

Raw, crude materials came together; men of the same level, as regarded education and station, took suddenly the different positions of masters and men, owing to the mother-wit, as regarded opportunities and probabilities, which distinguished some, and made them far-seeing as to what great future lay concealed in that rude model of Sir Richard Arkwright's. The rapid development of . . . a new trade, gave those early masters enormous power of wealth and command. I don't mean merely over the workmen; I mean over purchasers—over the whole world's market.

Speaking of the steam-hammer, Nasymth's invention, he said: 'this practical realisation of a gigantic thought, came out of one man's brain. . . . That very man has it within him to mount step by step, on each wonder he achieves to higher marvels still . . . we have many among us who, if he were gone, could spring into the breach and carry on the war which compels, and shall compel, all material power to yield to science'. However, a bitter strike, which she vividly describes, ultimately cripples Thornton's business. The leader of the strike is the father of a consumptive girl whom Margaret Hale, the principle character in the story, has been drawn to out of compassion. Thus, she contributes to bringing Thornton and the strike leader to an understanding, just as she had come to find a link with the workers of Manchester on the ground of common humanity. Thornton's mellowed attitude and

Cotton operatives in Manchester at the time of the Cotton
Famine, 1862–3.

composure in misfortune, the harsh edge of his personality being softened by his experiences, finally lead to Margaret's coming to love and marry him and, incidentally, save his business. The writer's message is 'we have all of us one human heart'.

When on holiday with Sir James Kay-Shuttleworth, the great education and health reformer, and his wife, in the Lake District she met and became a friend of Charlotte Bronte. In 1857 she produced Charlotte's biography. It received a mixed reception, but is still valued even today. From 1861 she wrote for the *Cornhill Magazine* and became a close friend of Gerge Smith the publisher. She continued writing up to the time of her death. *Cousin Phillis* contains fine rural landscape descriptions; *Sylvia's Lovers*, set at Whitby, deals with whalers, sailors and the press-gang. It contains both pathos and romance, contrasting personalities, and dramatic irony. Some of the best descriptions of rural ways occur in this novel. *Wives and Daughters*, not quite finished when Mrs Gaskell died, has a similar setting to *Cranford*. But it has a real plot. It contains evidences of sympathetic insights and dramatic power that have been held to foreshadow yet greater achievements had she lived. Both these latter works culminate in a reconciliation through tragedy.

It is hard to believe that she worked her literary life into the busy round of a mother and hostess. Her letters reveal her deep, almost modern involvement in her children's interests. Only a small part of her correspondence survives. This alone must have occupied her much. Her house was often packed with guests, sometimes famous ones like Dickens and Carlyle. She organised her staff of servants, ran a garden, latterly including a hen-house, a cow and pigs! She was active in Chapel work, Sunday Schools and other social welfare activities. At the time of the cotton famine in 1862 to 1863 she remarked that she was 'too worn out to eat anything or do anything but go to bed'. Much of her income from writing she put into the Relief Fund.

She enjoyed lighter moments at Lindeth Tower, an old defensive 'peel', near Silverdale. There the family stayed for six weeks, becoming 'strong as horses'. She could see the 'train of

Bust of Elizabeth Gaskell before her marriage.

crossers' led over the deadly sands by the guide. She loved the informal life. 'I have had to dine 15 people, as hungry as hounds, on shrimps & bread & butter'. Food had to be carried across an open court to be cooked. Her letters and lesser literary works are well worth reading for the glimpses they give of contemporary life and of earlier traditions, in which she was especially interested. Yet she was extremely wide in her interests. Writing of the things best worth seeing in Manchester she mentioned spinning mills, brickworks, machinery and railway engine works! Fascinating, too, are her detailed letters about her many tours.

Some woman! At 55 she died too soon. But could she have packed more variety into a longer life?

William Hesketh Lever, 1st Viscount Leverhulme, Emperor of Industry, 1851–1925

'The conduct of a successful business,' the undergraduates of Liverpool University were told in 1922, 'merely consists of doing things in a very simple way, doing them regularly and never neglecting to do them.'

The man who spoke these words had made his name a household word and the influence of the business empire he established was to extend yet wider after his death by a significant merger with the Dutch-based Margarine Union. Today soap and ice cream, toiletries and sausages, fish and margarine, fresh, canned and frozen foods may come to us by grace of one of the 500 companies of the Unilever combine. The plantations of the raw materials, the communities where the employees live, the ships which carry the material over many oceans, are also part of this empire, created by one man. He had able helpers, but it was part of his genius to pick out ability early, and all were inspired by the drive and energy of their chief, William Hesketh Lever.

'My happiness,' he once said, 'is my business. I can see finality for myself ... but none for my business. There one has room to breath, to grow, to expand, and the possibilities are boundless. One can go to places like the Congo and organise, organise, organise, well, very big things indeed. But I don't work at business only for the sake of money. I'm not a lover of money as money and never have been. I work at business because business is life. It enables me to do things.' By this he meant much more than selling 370,000 metric tons of soap throughout the world, directing a business which had then capital of over £64 million, and employed 85,000 people in many countries of the world. He had a vision of the active and prosperous community. He was keen to turn it into reality. Every fresh experience in his life seemed to generate new ideas for bringing this about.

Sir William Lever speaking on the occasion of his elevation to the Peerage in 1917.

73

His aim was thus simple; so was his method. He felt that business was his calling, he had a flair for it and by means of that business he wanted to enable the maximum number of people to enjoy the good life. Lever had definite ideas about what was the good life. It wasn't everybody's idea. Lever was naive ever to think so. Yet he pressed on. What is remarkable is that he tried to achieve so much and so largely succeeded.

To trace his life is an exhausting exercise. He went round the world five times, to say nothing of shorter trips. He left 30,000 files of letters. He skimped nothing, shirked nothing, and answered all letters personally—his 'simple way'. The older he grew the more his energy showed itself. During the last few years of his life he rose at 4 a.m., did his exercises, had a cold bath, digested business reports before breakfast at 7.30, and was at his

The plaque being unveiled at Lord Leverhulme's birthplace in Bolton 1970.

office often before 8.30, the official starting time. Throughout the year he slept under a glass veranda. He had one built in all his houses. He kept to one style of dress for speed and ease. At the age of 69 he took up dancing keenly. He said it kept him young and attracted young friends. At work he often had three stenographers taking at once so that nothing was missed! He never paused in dictation. Likewise, he seemed to make his business decisions almost instantaneously. On his trips abroad, he filled out every minute, taking younger executives with him, so that, while they widened their knowledge of the business world, he really got to know them. He would turn train, ship or car into an office if necessary.

This was his life—ever seeking wider horizons. 'A rut', he said, 'is like a grave, only longer'. Yet he admitted to being driven by fear, fear that he might let his shareholders down, fear that made him rise so early, even in the last year of his life. He showed his humanity in this, yet it was a strange sentiment. What was the background of this phenomenon of a man?

He was the first son, after six daughters, of devout Congregationalist parents who lived in the pleasant Georgian cul-de-sac called Wood Street in Bolton. It was a typical Victorian household, not excessively strict, simply insistent on profitable use of the time. They were very fond of concerts. He always held up his parents as models of their kind and paid tribute both to their principles and their affection and support. As a boy he was quick-witted, resourceful and orderly-minded, diligent though not outstanding at school. Many of his school friendships were life-long.

His father had a thriving wholesale grocery business, Lever & Co. William became apprenticed to his father, and began by cutting up soap! He progressed to the office. There he persuaded his father to have the accounts system made more efficient, using an accountant's advice. This was only the first of many 'bright ideas' which transformed a small firm into a worldwide business. Yet, though he reacted against his father's business conservatism, he imitated his father's deep involvement in the affairs of his workpeople. We may call it paternalism. He would have called it fatherly interest. So loyal

were his father's men that they offered to take lower wages when business was bad!

Like many great men, William hated idleness. His hobbies were carpentry and natural history rambles. He loved Shakespeare and Dickens and quotable humour, such as that of W. S. Gilbert. On his sixteenth birthday he was given a copy of Smiles' *Self-Help*, to which he constantly referred. A regular churchgoer and a daily reader of the Bible all his life, like his father, he venerated the Bible as a mine of practical truths. 'If a businessman has not read the book of Proverbs', he once declared, 'I will never believe that he can be a true, careful, sound and cautious businessman'. He never once gambled, not even for the fun of it. The sight of the inside of the Monte Carlo Casino nauseated him, principally because he regarded the winning of an unearned fortune as degrading. Family life was run economically but not stingily. William recorded enjoyable visits to Fountains Abbey and to the stately homes of Derbyshire in 1869. Here he showed the beginnings of his passionate interest in historic architecture. His school friend, Jonathan Simpson, who became an architect, was to help to cultivate this enthusiasm.

At 19 William went on the road and at 21 he was taken into partnership at the generous salary, then, of £800 a year. He was married to his childhood sweetheart in 1874. He surprised people by the alterations he made to his first home. But this was an omen, for he constantly altered, adapted and improved his various homes and everything he touched. William was responsible for extending the firm's territory to the Wigan district and opening a Wigan warehouse. This too was an omen. He was always to be looking for fresh customers. He thought of other improvements in the business. In 1885 he produced *The Lancashire Grocer* for circulation among customers. He began to advertise. Lever & Co. became the largest wholesale grocers outside Manchester and Liverpool.

Since 1874 Lever & Co., had sold a soap known as 'Lever's pure honey soap'. In 1875 the Trade Marks Act was passed. Young William saw the possibilities. Why not persuade people, as incomes rose, to buy more soap, his soap, just as he had caused them to buy more butter in the past? Now it was possible to have a trade name that no

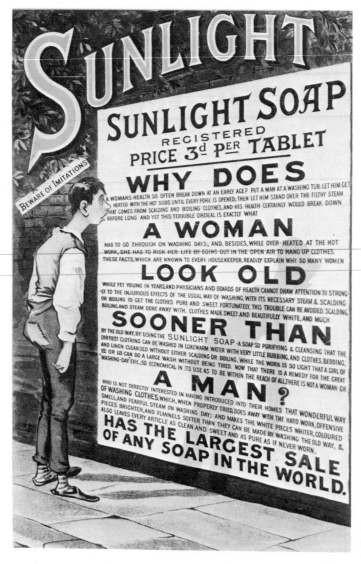

An early advertisement for Sunlight Soap, 1888.

one else could use, round which one could 'put a halo' as he later described it. A trade mark agent suggested the name 'Sunlight' to him. It clicked! He got it registered at once.

Originally the name covered a range of soaps made by various firms. But William Lever's favourite was the 'Self Washer', a vegetable oil soap, in contrast to most others which were based on animal fat. But there were manufacturing problems. At the same time, raw material prices were falling. William thought this was a signal to begin manufacturing. Lever senior's view was: 'A cobbler should stick to his last'. However, William got the necessary loans and bought the soap works of Winser & Co., at Warrington. This firm, though then running at a loss, had men in it who provided the technical expertise to match William Lever's sales drive and organising ability. Thus by 1888 Sunlight soap was the best selling soap in Britain.

From 20 tons in 1886 to 250 tons a week in 1887, the expansion continued. They were making all the soap the factory could produce. Despite obstruction by bankers and landlords, William Lever still pressed on. His sales spread overseas. 'I let it grow in this way.'

In early summer, 1887, he had been scouring both sides of the Mersey. Eventually, on the Cheshire side, amid open fields and marshes, between railway and river, where land was still cheap, he looked over a gate and said: 'Here we are'. He bought 52 acres. He already had the scheme of an industrial village in his mind. He named it Port Sunlight. His wife cut the first sod for the new factory in March 1888. At the subsequent banquet in Liverpool he expressed the hope that he would soon be able 'to build houses in which our workpeople will be able to live and be comfortable . . . in which they will be able to know more about the science of life than they can in a back slum, and in which they will learn that there is more enjoyment in life than in the mere going to and returning from work and looking forward to Saturday night to draw their wages'.

In the first full year of production at Port Sunlight, 1889, 15,688 tons of soap were produced. How was the market obtained? Lever (from now on William is the 'Lever') used a vast range of advertising stunts. One of his first hinged on the slogan: 'Why does a woman look old sooner than a man?' The answer given was because she stood so long by her steaming washtub! With Sunlight soap, she had a quicker and better wash! Lever issued a booklet with the soap. Poetry was written:

> 'Twill make your brow a snowy white,
> As free from grief and care,
> As when with youth your eyes were bright
> And cheeks beyond compare,
> This article, if you but try,
> Will realise each hope,
> Go send your maid at once, and buy
> A box of Sunlight soap.

Like Pears, he used well-known paintings. He introduced prize schemes and the profusely illustrated *Sunlight Year Book*, which was used in schools! Other soap manufacturers, who held that each soap maker should have his own 'area',

resented this aggressive sales promotion. Lever encouraged competition amongst his salesmen. One keen man conducted a survey at a wedding at which he was a guest, by which he proved conclusively the superiority of Sunlight soap!

Thus the firm expanded. Like the admiral of a fleet, Lever, from his central office, raised like a bridge of a ship, organised operations. But he never forgot his wider aims. He rejected profit-sharing. He felt that a better way of benefiting most workers was not to give them more money but better conditions, such as good houses at low rents. The whole Port Sunlight philosophy he called 'prosperity-sharing'. In 1891 he asked Gladstone over to open the Gladstone Hall, the first village institution in Port Sunlight. Lever, a staunch Liberal, was tremendously impressed by Gladstone. Also, the prestige imparted by the great man's visit gave a boost to shares and sales.

The very unpromising nature of the terrain at Port Sunlight was a challenge to Lever. He loved altering and adapting. He loved making wide roads lined with trees. The houses were well spaced out, with varied designs, many being replicas of fine houses, such as Shakespeare's Birthplace in Stratford. Thus Lever indulged his love of architecture. There were schools, a theatre, library, hospital, in fact every recreational and cultural facility; finally, by popular request, a 'local'. In 1902 he erected a Gothic church, to serve all denominations. Though a Congregationalist, he loved the traditional style of the English parish church. In 1913 the foundation stone of the Lady Lever Art Gallery was laid by George V. Owing to the war it was not completed until 1922. It contains pictures, sculptures, tapestries, ceramics and fine furniture. Lever loved the visual arts and helped artists generously. From 1887 he acquired many important pictures, building up a fine and large collection, most of the best of which are in the Gallery.

Lever was accused of paternalism, of course. But it is hard to see how a man who has spent a great deal to create a happy community, could be expected to allow his provisions to be marred or frittered away by neglect or improvidence. That Port Sunlight was in the main a success is proved by the well attested good spirit, efficiency and good health of the working community there. The trade unionist who wrote that 'no men of independent turn of mind can breathe long the atmosphere of Port Sunlight ... The system ... makes (the workers) servile and sycophant, it lowers them to the level of machines tending machines,' was surely expressing an extreme viewpoint.

Lever's attitude is summed up in his own words:

No employer-capitalist with a true feeling of brotherhood can be quite happy ... in the enjoyment of wealth (the product of his own hard work) ... without feeling a strong sense of dissatisfaction with present industrial conditions and a strong desire to improve them so that the employee-workman may be raised to a much higher level in social well-being.

In the old days a manufactory would be an individual

Meanwhile the business was being yet further enlarged. Lever visited the States in 1888, gleaning many new ideas there. He made his first voyage round the world in 1892. In 1894 Lifebuoy Soap was launched, followed in 1899 by Monkey Brand, the product of an American company he took over, and Lux soap flakes. The reason behind the mergers which took place, after some difficulties, Lever put thus:

concern. Next a partnership ... then limited companies ... that a still larger capital may be got together. Now we have reached a further stage ... limited companies required to be group together in ... a combine, the object being the concentration of capital and the concentration of effort; if these combines result in cheaper production and more abundant supply, (these) undertakings will be successful.

A pleasant house near the Factory at Port Sunlight model village, c. 1900.

By 1920 Crosfields, Price's Candles, Gibbs and Knights of Castile soap fame were all in the Lever group, as well as many other soap firms well-known in their day.

The high price of raw materials induced Lever to try to produce his own. He began in the Solomon Islands, but his great venture was in the Belgian Congo. Lever had the personal support of King Albert himself and in 1911 he virtually established industrial principalities in five areas of palm-bearing land. He was empowered to build roads and railways, in fact to provide every social facility. He bought companies trading with Africa, and shipping lines. His acquisition of the Niger Company brought him involvements from which only the brilliant financial brain of Francis D'Arcy Cooper, the eminent accountant, extricated him. Cooper succeeded as chairman on Lever's death.

One might have thought that with these preoccupations alone, even Lever's mental energies would be fully engaged. But, in 1917, in the island of Lewis and Harris in the Outer Hebrides, he saw a new field of activity. Houses, roads and commercial facilities were under-developed. He bought the island, began to organise the tweed and fishing industries, improved port facilities, in short he set about bringing all the benefits of modern life to these remote areas. He bought a chain of fish shops, now known as MacFisheries, to market the fish, as well as other fishing concerns. But in Lewis, despite much initial support, his schemes foundered, largely owing to the deep-rooted independent spirit of the crofter. In Harris, however, he got further. Leverburgh still perpetuates his name. (Ironically, many of the policies he advocated are now being employed by those concerned today in the development of the Scottish highlands and islands.)

It is an equal wonder that he squeezed politics into his life as well. He was something of a philosopher in his own way and he expounded his views and practices to a wide range of audiences. Incidentally, he became quite a popular speaker, with his Lancashire accent, dialect stories and graphic illustrations of his points. He was a committed Liberal, seeing both the selfishness of many capitalists and the shortsightedness of much Left-wing talk. Prejudice and class-distinction he abhorred. From 1892 he stood for Parliament, first for Birkenhead, then for Wirral. In 1906 he was elected. He made significant speeches on old age pensions and the payment of M.P.'s. In 1911 he was created a baronet. In 1917 he was raised to the peerage as Lord Leverhulme of Bolton-le-Moors. His first speech in the Lords was in favour of a decimal coinage system the basis of which was the halfpenny, a hundred of which would make one 'royal' and five 'royals' a guinea. He saw things from the point of view of the housewife, his main customer; he realised that the use of decimals of the pound would cause inflation. A prophet indeed!

In 1919 he spoke on industrial unrest. He believed that better education, to remove misunderstanding on both sides, was the answer. He recalled his youth among the cotton operatives. Lord Curzon, a Conservative, wrote that he had delivered 'one of the finest speeches . . . for years'. In 1922 he was created Viscount Leverhulme of the Western Isles.

For Bolton, his native town, he had special affection. He built a Congregational Church there in memory of his parents. Hall-i'th'Wood, a Tudor house associated with Crompton, he restored and gave to Bolton as a museum. The fine buildings of Bolton School today are but part of his gift to that school. He bought the Rivington estate, including the Pike, the beacon tower, and the fine medieval barn. There he laid out gardens, walks, pools and streams on the slopes. Much of the estate he gave to the public as a park. In 1913 his bungalow there was burnt by a suffragette. Ironically, he had spoken for women's suffrage several times.

To Liverpool University, especially the School of Civic Design, Tropical Medicine and Russian studies, he gave the proceeds of a successful law case. Liverpool's most beautiful building, the old Blue Coat School, Lever saved from demolition. These are only a few of his academic and cultural endowments.

He held public offices in Lancashire and Cheshire. He was mayor of Bolton in 1918. His suggestions regarding rating were embodied in the Act of 1922. In 1924 Leverhulme put forward his own plans for Bolton's civic centre, which would be worthy of a town such as he envisaged

Bolton would eventually become. He offered to defray part of the cost himself. The scheme was rejected, to Bolton's loss.

His adopted village of Thornton Hough, where he had bought the manor, he practically rebuilt, including the old smithy before which he planted—a chestnut tree! His love of wide, straight roads can be seen in the approach to the village, and here again he built a Congregational church, using the classic Norman style.

Much of his public work is perforce omitted. His work in the 1914–18 war is a story in itself.

He died in harness. Shortly before he died, presiding at the annual meeting of Lever Brothers, he defended his business record. His last public appearance was an address to the scholars of the Sunday school of the church he built at Bolton. He took ill the next day, dying on Thursday. He lies beside his wife in the church he built at Port Sunlight.

One day he was planning a new drive to Thornton Manor. Taking a ruler, he drew a straight line from Port Sunlight to the manor. This was his method—'a very simple way'. All challenges he surmounted in the spirit of his tutor, Smiles, believing that they were there to be overcome and turned to account. A naive belief, perhaps. But it spells disaster for humanity if it has died with him.

L. S. Lowry, Artist of Industrial Life, Born 1887

Lowry is as Lowry paints. He is still alive, though he was born in 1887 at Old Trafford, Manchester. He was an only child. His father was an Estate Agent, 'a very sober, punctual man. My mother was altogether different. She was a very able pianist . . . she had a wonderful eye for beautiful things. I have her collection of old china and clocks. She did not understand my painting, but she understood me and that was enough'. Early in his life the family moved to the smartish suburb of Rusholme. He was educated at Victoria Park School from 1895 to 1904. From 1908 to 1915 he studied drawing and painting at Manchester College of Art, after which he attended the Salford School of Art, on and off, till 1925.

Meanwhile, in 1909, his parents moved to Station Road, Pendlebury, part of the slightly less concentrated urban sprawl that, pock-marked with coal pits and industrial premises, lies between Manchester and Bolton. There he lived for nearly 40 years. From 1915 to 1920 he became more interested in the artistic possibilities of his own area and there we can discern the genesis of his mature themes. But he never passed any examinations or seriously attempted to get a regular job. His parents sustained him during this lean period. He never married. His father lived till 1932, long enough however, to see one of the paintings of his son, *An Accident,* (1926), accepted by a public gallery, the Manchester City Art Gallery, in 1930. In that year too, on the invitation of the author Harold Timperley, a friend of his, Lowry illustrated *A Cotswold Book* with pencil sketches. The year of his father's death Lowry first exhibited at the Royal Academy, where since 1956 he has exhibited regularly until recently. In 1938 he was 'discovered'. Just by chance Alex Reid, a partner in the Reid & Lefevre Gallery in London, saw a Lowry at the framers. He was fascinated. He

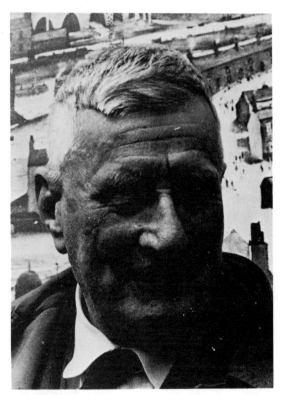

L. S. Lowry.

enquired who the artist was. He was told that Lowry's pictures were often sent to annual exhibitions but 'most come back'. The result was Lowry's first one-man show in London in 1939, at which the Tate Gallery bought his *Dwellings, Ordsall Lane, Salford*. The Lefevre Gallery act as his dealer and have held many exhibitions of his works. From that point on he never looked back.

In 1941, Salford City Art Gallery arranged an exhibition of his work. In 1945 he received an honorary M.A. from Manchester University. These were just the first of a rarely interrupted succession of exhibitions, honours and, of course, profitable sales! In 1955 he became an Associate of the Royal Academy and in 1962 a full Royal Academician. In 1951 Maurice Collis wrote the first book about him, and in 1957 B.B.C. Television made a film of his life. In 1965 he received the freedom of the City of Salford, and in 1966 he was chosen 'Man of the Year' by the Manchester Junior Chamber of Commerce. Also, a large retrospective exhibition of his work, sponsored by the Arts Council, was held at the Tate Gallery.

What sort of person is this bachelor artist, belatedly recognised at the age of 52? He is not anti-social, cynical, an anarchist, layabout or a Bohemian. He can talk stocks and shares, admires the great industrialists, especially the pioneers, the 'masters' of men, who built and maintained businesses by their own hard work and commanded respect, in contrast to the vast impersonal organisations of today. He hates change, even in respect of things he dislikes. He wears the same sort of clothes every day. His paintings usually portray figures in the dress of the 1920s, but latterly he does not hesitate to depict the fashions of modern youth. He also hates his house in Mottram, to which he moved in 1948, nine years after his mother died, but cannot face the unsettlement of leaving.

He embodies the culture of the great days of the Liberal party, historically identified with Manchester and Free Trade, epitomised by the Manchester Guardian and C. P. Scott, Miss Horniman's Repertory Theatre and the Hallé. He loves music, especially Italian Opera. He likes and admires the art of the Pre-Raphaelites, as well as Turner, Sargent and Munnings. A life-long Manchester City supporter, he has also keenly followed Rugby League and has a memory of cricket spanning three quarters of a century. Like many Lancashire folk, he has a strong sense of humour, indeed he loves to make gentle fun of people. He keeps stressing his inborn laziness: 'Perhaps that is why I have been so industrious all my life'. Thus, he advises young people: 'don't be an artist!' He admires those who give it up for something more remunerative, or less arduous but, of course, his tongue is well in his cheek. Now that success has come to him he has been asked what he feels like when a picture of his is re-sold for many times its original price. He says he feels like a horse when he hears that his jockey has won the prize. On a deeper level, he has an underlying religious sense. 'Nature doesn't waste anything . . . I just can't believe it will all come to nothing in the end'.

His house contains many objects his mother collected, and those he has collected, including 14 clocks, 'wonderful companions' all ticking away in their own time. He lives in traditional bachelor style, rather cluttered, with piles of unopened mail. Except for breakfast he has every meal out, usually in Manchester. He frequently goes to Sunderland and used to visit London, although he scorns those who regard living in London as necessary for success. He is a lone character, but hardly lonely. He has always had a number of friends and his very approachable. He enjoys company and has made new friends even in old age. He takes an interest in local schools and often helps art students.

'Will I live?' he asks modestly. He constantly pays tribute to his first teacher of drawing, Adolphe Valette, who also introduced him to the techniques of the Impressionists. Lowry is a fine draughtsman. He learnt the traditional way. His early portrait drawings and paintings, which include portraits of his parents in 1910, show some competence. He painted his first landscape in 1909, showing a fondness for white which has grown on him. He executed a series of Fylde landscapes in 1918 reminiscent of the Impressionists. It was the play *Hindle Wakes* which drew his attention to the tragi-comic poetry of the lives of industrial workers and their families around him. He had been for some time absorbing the local scene, after overcoming his initial

L. S. Lowry—a self-portrait, 1925.

revulsion. He observed the conditions described so well by Robert Roberts in *Salford—The Classic Slum*. It was a time of Depression, too. Lowry realised that no one had ever portrayed the industrial scene with true sympathy. By 1919, the characteristic Lowry scene begins to appear. In 1921 his work was exhibited in an architect's office in Manchester. There his pastel *The Lodging House* was sold, for £5. Perhaps it was then that his father warned him not to get bigheaded! The review in the *Manchester Guardian* by Bernard Taylor, later a great friend, ran thus:

A very interesting and individual outlook . . . with real imagination. . . . He emphasises . . . everything that industrialism has done to make the aspect of Lancashire more forbidding than that of most other places. . . . His Lancashire is grey, with vast rectangular mills towering over diminutive houses . . . the crowds which have this landscape for their background are entirely in keeping with their setting: the incidents in the drama of which they are the characters are also appropriate 'A Labour Exchange', 'The Entrance for Outpatients' . . . The artist's technique is not yet equal to his ideas. If he can learn to express himself with ease and style and at the same time preserve his singleness of outlook, he may make a real contribution to art.

That promise has been amply fulfilled. Lowry has worked hard and long over the years, developing his style and techniques. Now he has lived long enough to receive his reward. These early pictures are very dark but Mr Taylor pointed out to Lowry that the industrial scene was not really dark. Lowry realised that this was so. Lord Clark speaks of mills floating 'in a perpetual, pearly mist'. The sky effects and the delicate use of tone in his depiction of buildings, which is particularly apparent in his rendering of different materials and his representation of distance, illustrate Lowry's mastery of the use of white.

Originally, Lowry drew every figure in detail, but not only does this call for a disproportionate amount of work but fails to give the impression of a moving, mingling, shifting crowd, which over the years Lowry has made his speciality. His earlier figures are like jointed dolls. The animation is latent. But by 1924 the movement has become free. The painting, *An Accident*, based on an actual incident in a croft behind his house

where a girl drowned herself in a pond, illustrates these points. Buildings recede like ghosts into the background smog. Chimneys and domes spike the sky. A crowd is growing from its original nucleus. Old folk, housewives, workmen, children, are moving, having moved, or are about to move, motivated by the dominant concern. Over all tower the great chimneys, all belching smoke, and all around are endless ranks of dwellings. Only tragedy breaks the monotony of the life of the 'faceless ones'.

Lowry has depths of pathos, the pathos of loneliness, of strain, of the misfit, of the odd one out. This appears in paintings like *Head of a Man with Red Eyes*, (1936), *The Cripples*, (1949), *Man Lying on a Wall*, (1957), and many others; also in his pictures of lonely houses, possibly haunted, such as *An Island*, (1942), his unbroken *Seascape*, (1952), and even more in his endless *The Lakes*, (1950). In his self portrait, too, in 1925, he looks anxiously at himself, wondering what the future holds. In the 1920s unemployment was high; if he had wanted a job would there be one for him and who would buy his paintings? He is dressed for the road, He cannot escape from the outside world. His only hope is to explore it, on foot, in the hope of discovering its poetry.

'I wanted to paint myself into what absorbed me. . . . Had I not been lonely I should not have seen what I did'. Of his figures he has said, 'They are symbols of my mood . . . they are myself . . . Natural figures would have broken the spell, so I made them half unreal. . . . All those people in my pictures . . . have got their private sorrows, but they can't contact one another . . . crowds are the most lonely thing of all'.

Yet, being Lancashire, he and his characters do not mope. They can laugh at themselves and their plight. Lowry has been described as a collector stalking human insects with his net. But he does not mount them in a pretty case like butterflies. He shows us the whole live anthill. The crowd cuts a comic figure. The faces and poses of running, squabbling and sprawling children, loungers and pushers, old men with sticks and ladies with prams, some in knots and some alone, fascinate like Brueghel's peasants In the pictures exhibited in the 1921 show and later, in paintings like *The*

'An Accident' by L. S. Lowry, 1926.

Fight and many others, we are given a closer look still.

Yet there are brighter sides to life in the industrial city. There are parks and Art Galleries even in Salford, Gothic Revival Churches, iron lamp stands, wakes and fairs, as well as football matches and regattas at Agecroft. Lowry's painting *Daisy Nook on Good Friday* is as full of brightness as some of his seaside scenes. The roundabouts are in full swing, every child has a windmill or a balloon, everyone meets their friends, in fact, apart from the mill on the horizon you forget that it is all taking place in a Manchester suburb. Deep down, maybe, the shimmering crowd have lonely hearts, but they still get on with living. Life is not so bad. Once Lowry went to a clairvoyant. He told her he was a lonely old man without a friend in the world. She told him that it was not so and proceeded to describe one of his closest friends very accurately. 'There is a lot in clairvoyance, you know. I am sure of it!'

Lowry too has many-sided genius. His 26 sketches for his first one-man exhibition, at the Manchester University Settlement, in 1930 illustrate his excellence as a topographical artist. Many aspects of the rapidly vanishing townscape of industrial Lancashire have been brilliantly recorded by his brush and pen. Many of his commissioned works are outstanding. Has any artist ever portrayed human expressions better than Lowry has in his *The Out-Patients Department, Ancoats Hospital?*

Lowry has made the industrial landscape his own, not only in Lancashire but in many other industrial areas. He has produced fine paintings of South Wales and of Tyne and Wear. His interest in the Fylde landscape has recurred from time to time. His port and ship, beach and sea pictures, such as *The Liver Buildings, Liverpool,* and *The Royal Iris* are masterpieces too. His seascapes afford scope for his theme of alone-ness, as we have already noticed.

His advice to all aspiring artists is: 'Paint the

85

'Out-patients' department, Ancoats Hospital, Manchester' by L. S. Lowry.

place you know—the place where you belong'. This is what he himself has done. In the words of Lord Clark: 'He first responds to what he sees, irrespective of what it represents and then broods sympathetically on the result'. In the words of Miss Carol Kroch:

There is no romantic pretension to preach the rigours of hard times in the North to the South. They are principally depictions of what and how, in accordance with his own temperament, he has observed, always with an artist's fascination, often with mischievous amusement, and frequently with a deeply felt compassion for the abandoned and helpless, in a lifetime spent in a particular environment. You, the observer can interpret them according to your own temperament. For that is what art is all about: the cultivation, enrichment and heightening of sensibility.

The eminent contributors to the festschrift of 1964 on his 77th birthday, all witness to his originality and sensitivity. The late Gerald Cotton, sometime Borough Librarian of Swinton, wrote:

Lowry . . . embraces a complete regional culture . . . The apparent simplicity of Lowry's style is . . . one of the most remarkable compressions of visual and emotional experience . . . he has retained the freshness of a child's view of life.

To quote Miss Kroch again:

Lowry is a 'man of his time', who has recorded life as he saw it with such basic humanity in his best works that they will enlist the sympathy of all times and all societies.

Kathleen Ferrier, The More than Golden Voice, 1912–1953

In the 1930's people in Blackburn made telephone calls just for the pleasure of hearing the operator's voice. That voice was to become known the world over. The owner of the voice was Kathleen Ferrier, 'Katie' to Sir John Barbirolli, 'Kath' to many others, 'Klever Kaff' when on top of her form!

Her father, of Pembrokeshire ancestry, though his mother was Lancashire, was a teacher. So was her mother, and descended from Scottish and Ulster stock. Both were musically gifted. From her mother Kathleen derived her irrespressible sense of fun and a dauntless ambition; from her father she inherited the reserves of patience needed to make a naturally good voice into a great voice.

She was born in Higher Walton, a mill village between Preston and Blackburn, on 22nd April, 1912. But very soon Mrs Ferrier felt the need to be near the superior educational facilities of Blackburn. On her urging, father Ferrier applied for and got the headship of St Paul's School, Blackburn, to which the family moved in 1914.

From an early age Kathleen showed a natural ability to entertain. She also tended to assume she could achieve anything if she really wanted. She virtually taught herself to read before she went to school. She began picking out tunes on the piano by ear at the age of three or four. A friend bought her a piano tutor and taught her the names of the notes. She taught herself to read music. Her mother, convinced that she had real talent, sought out the best possible teacher, Frances Walker, famous in the north of England for the musical achievements of her pupils. She did not usually take beginners, but she took Kathleen.

As a schoolgirl Kathleen sang in tune, but huskily. She was happy at school, a quick learner, a keen Girl Guide, fond of a lark, good at impersonating and a mistress of facial manipulation.

Kathleen Ferrier.

It looked as though she would become one of the many great pianists who were growing up in Lancashire at that time. Kathleen was usually among the top four at music festivals.

The Ferrier parents lived frugally to pay for their children's education. Elder sister Winifred went to college, but brother George was rather a disappointment and money might be needed to help him out. In 1926, too, it was a time of depression, the year of the General Strike. It was decided that Kathleen must leave school and enter the Post Office. Kathleen had to make the best of it. She learnt how to bear up and see humour in routine activities.

Her uncle and cousins also provided scope for family musical activity. After Kathleen had sung at a family performance, her mother said: 'I believe our Kath's going to have a contralto voice. I love a contralto'.

When only 14 she passed the final grade of the Associated Board examinations, 'an unprecedented success' said a newspaper. In 1928 she won a piano in the northern region of a national piano playing contest run by the Daily Express. However, at the final contest in London, her first trip to the capital, Kathleen was nervous and was not among the winning six. But Miss Walker sent a reassuring telegram: 'You've done your best'. Kathleen was to do that all her life.

She continued to perform, winning more prizes and taking the A.R.C.M. and L.R.A.M. diplomas. On the 3rd July, 1930 she broadcast for the first time as a pianist in a concert at the Manchester studios. She joined a church choir in Blackburn. In a performance of *Elijah* in 1931, she was chosen to sing in the trio 'Lift thine eyes'. The local paper reported that she sang 'pleasingly . . . more will be heard in Blackburn of this young vocalist'. In her piano playing she was also showing that intensity of insight and emotion which was to mark her singing.

About 1935 the Golden Voice contest for the G.P.O. speaking clock was held. Kathleen competed but just failed to win. But she still wanted to use her voice. In 1935 she entered the Blackpool Festival in the Tudor class, both singing and playing her own accompaniment. She had taken singing lessons in preparation. But she did not even receive an honourable mention!

In 1935, too, she married a young bank clerk, but it was an unfortunate match, later to be dissolved. However, her husband's job took her to Silloth, in Cumberland. There the small son of a friend of hers nicknamed her 'Klever Kaff', for sewing on a button quickly! The name took her fancy.

In March 1937 she entered the Carlisle Festival as a pianist and just for the fun of it, as a contralto soloist. This was the turning point. She not only won the trophy for piano playing but also the Silver Rose Bowl as the best singer of the Festival. It was Maurice Jacobson who told her that her voice was one of the finest he had heard and that she should make singing her career.

At the Millom Festival she sang *Secrecy* by Hugo Wolf. The adjudicator said: 'A beautiful voice, full of colour and lovely warm velvety quality . . . it makes me imagine I am being stroked'.

She first broadcast as a singer in 1939. She sang *Curly Headed Babby*, *Mighty Like a Rose* and, with the Millom male voice choir, *The End Of A Perfect Day*. In April '39 she entered for the Carlisle Festival again. She sang a difficult work, *All Souls' Day* by Richard Strauss. Doctor Hutchinson adjudicated and said: 'a real contralto, with a most artistic conception of the song'. The outbreak of war brought Dr Hutchinson to Keswick. This was the opportunity Kathleen had been waiting for. He became her teacher. For three and a half years they worked together. Between them they smoothed out the defects in her voice control, a mutual quest for perfection which took 18 months until, to quote her sister Winifred: 'the lovely voice was poised securely throughout its compass—two octaves from bottom G to top G'. She built up a repertoire which included Purcell, Bach's *B Minor Mass*, the *Saint John* and *Saint Matthew Passions*, many older Italian arias, all the Handel Oratorios and Elgar's *Dream of Gerontius*. Dr Hutchinson commented: 'what a joy to direct such gifts but what a responsibility!'

During the war her singing cheered people all over Britain. In 1942 she sang to Dr Malcolm Sargent. He told her she had a great future if she was prepared to live in London. He put her in touch with a well-known firm of London concert agents. They gave her an audition and engaged her on the spot. She was now, 14 years after her

Kathleen Ferrier's birthplace in Higher Walton.

Kathleen Ferrier accompanied by Gerald Moore at Carlisle.

unsuccessful piano final in London, there again, as a professional musician now, with a London manager.

So Winifred secured a post and a flat in London for Kathleen and their father; their mother had died just before Kathleen's first broadcast. A publicity leaflet was produced for her with a quotation from the *Manchester Guardian*, by the critic Granville Hill:

Miss Kathleen Ferrier, a new singer of remarkable talent, was heard yesterday in the Houldsworth Hall, Manchester. A full, rich contralto voice, flexible throughout its compass and capable of lovely shades of tone and expression, is rare in these days . . . she sings with feeling and intelligence, using her vocal gifts as the servant of her temperament.

He did, however, remark that she needed to make sure that her words were always clear and to attain greater consistency in tone-shading. A Liverpool paper compared her to Clara Butt.

She was never short of engagements now. Her reputation and repertoire grew. Yet she still wished for a teacher. She approached Roy Henderson. It was he who helped her to memorise, to be confident and 'look right' even when evincing great feeling.

In 1943 she sang in Westminster Abbey, the first time she had sung the *Messiah* in London. Isobel Baillie was the soprano. Peter Pears also made his debut then. 'Natural dignity' and 'purity' commented the *Musical Times*. Dr Jaques, the conductor, wrote that 'he was electrified, not only by the natural beauty of her voice but by the glowing sincerity of the whole performance. Kathleen had a way of getting to the heart of the music which was inimitable'. It was but the first of Kathleen's engagements with the Bach Choir. 'Always cheerful, happy and co-operative.'

In 1944 she sang in Manchester again. Granville Hill found no fault with her enunciation this time. 'Tuppence to speak to me now', said Kathleen, recalling his earlier comments! 'The perpetual student lasts so much longer', was the advice given to Kathleen by a well-known singer. Kathleen had already grasped this truth.

As 1945 opened she was clearly in the front rank. She had a national reputation and had begun recording. Her voice, however, in early records had a hard 'edge'. The reviews, however, were good. She herself would have re-made nearly all of them.

At the Promenade Concert of September 1945 it was estimated that five million people heard her. *The Sunday Times* described her voice as 'of an international order'.

Among the audience at Westminster Abbey had been the composer Benjamin Britten. He was 'impressed immediately by the nobility and beauty of her presence and by the warmth and deep range of her voice'. He was writing the opera *The Rape of Lucretia*. Kathleen had hitherto not been attracted by any contralto operatic parts. She was however persuaded to take the part of Lucretia at Glyndebourne, the famous Sussex music centre. Kathleen put all her resources of genius and of resilient and zestful personality into this new role, with immense success. 'Now I'll be forever chaste', she sang. It was expressive of personal sadness. Her early marriage was to be annulled in 1947. It seemed to be a choice between marriage and music. She chose music. Often she was to speak wistfully of the joys that others had in family life, but they were not for her.

She was to make the part of Lucretia her own. In 1946 this role took her to Holland, where the opera roused much enthusiasm. This was her first visit abroad.

With the hectic routine of a travelling singer, it is not surprising that she burnt herself out at the age of 41. She could hardly bear to refuse a request. Overwork became normal. In 1947, after a visit to Belfast, she decided she must learn more *lieder*. Thanks to Hans Oppenheim she mastered them and became an enthusiast for Mahler. Oppenheim recalled that she was moved to tears by Mahler's music frequently.

Bruno Walter had been invited to conduct Mahler's *Song of the Earth* at the first Edinburgh Festival in 1947. He was introduced to Kathleen. These are his words:

. . . one of the greatest singers of our time; a voice of rare beauty, a natural production of tone, a genuine warmth of expression, an innate understanding of the musical phrase—a personality.

Thus began a most happy musical association.

This was a new departure and a real challenge.

So was the opera *Orfeo*, in Italian at Glyndebourne in which she played Orfeo. Sir Steuart Wilson wrote to Kathleen: 'your Orfeo is the nearest to the armchair dream most of us will ever see'. After a Devon holiday came Edinburgh and Mahler. With much practice she controlled the tears—not of sentimentality but of 'strength of feeling ... and a deep comprehension of another great heart', as Walter put it. *The Times* reported: '... the splendid singing of Miss Kathleen Ferrier, whose voice seemed to have gained an added richness and a power which surmounted the orchestral climaxes with ease'.

Engagements in Europe and America followed. Meanwhile she made her debut at Covent Garden as Lucretia. Within five years she had advanced from Carlisle to Covent Garden. 'Lucky Kath', she exclaimed to herself.

On New Year's day, 1948, she set sail for New York. There the critics' reception was mixed. Walter, however, was thrilled. The conductor, Stokowski, too, expressed his opinion: 'simply superb ... so full and beautiful, intonation always perfect, the phrasing so elastic, the interpretation so eloquent'. She arrived home just in time for the *Dream of Gerontius* at the Albert Hall the next day. Her life for the next three years reads like the schedule of an airline pilot. One can only pick out highlights. She sang Mahler at the Salzburg Festival. Critics in this shrine of music were happy. So were the orchestra, as their wild applause proved. In Paris the papers reported: 'this English singer conquered'. At Vienna, where she sang in the Bach Festival, the Society of the Friends of Music were enthralled. Her performance at La Scala, Milan, of the Bach Mass brought tears to many eyes. Her visit to Holland with Gerald Moore was the start of another partnership. He wrote of her 'sweet nature, ... un-prima-donnishness'.

In Britain she visited 250 different places. Whether she performed with amateurs or professionals she always gave her best, yet without any airs of greatness.

From 1948 on she worked increasingly with the late Sir John Barbirolli. He and she shared the same attitude to their art. They both loved good food and good fun and hated humbug. She sang practically all her favourite pieces with him. She found much happiness in the Barbirolli home.

In 1951 tragedy struck. She had an operation for cancer, followed by constant treatment. She celebrated her recovery from the operation at her favourite restaurant, the Casa Prada in Euston Road, where her signature graces the wall. Amid laughter, she opened a locket to show—her stitches! She took a holiday in Sussex where she relaxed in rambling and painting. This latter activity was her favourite hobby. A tourist saw her painting in Alfriston. 'Look', she said, 'a real live artist!'

When Kathleen reappeared in public, at the Albert Hall, *The Times* critic reported: 'Powers unimpaired'. Yet in her diary Kathleen wrote about this time: 'Feeling like death'.

The climax for Lancashire was achieved in November 1951, at the opening of the rebuilt Free Trade Hall in Manchester. There 'the most exquisite and resplendent Rose of Lancaster—our Katie' sang Elgar's *Land of Hope and Glory*.

By some alchemy of sincerity and inborn genius, she made the rather outmoded words seem not in the least incongruous and lifted the whole thing to a noble climax, which moved everyone, not least the conductor, to tears.

A great tribute from Sir John Barbirolli, a musician who adopted Lancashire, to the greatest Lancashire-born singer.

Even in her last year of activity her development continued. The late Sir Neville Cardus wrote of Sir John and Kathleen's performance of the *Gerontius* in London: it came as near to faultlessness as could be wished.

She seemed to know that she was about to finish her career. Poignant intensity marked her singing. She seemed to be almost preternaturally enabled to perform despite increasing illness. On New Year's eve 1952 she sang and laughed as gaily as ever. Yet though she felt the cold, soon became tired, suffered from 'rheumatiz', she joked, danced, and travelled and performed, as she was able, throughout most of that year.

A great occasion was the private party at which the Queen and Queen Mother were present. Her diary reads: 'Party marvellous. Sang and sang. Princess Margaret sang too. Memorable evening'. One midsummer day, staying with a fellow-musician, she danced on the lawn barefoot. Next door, the Royal Standard rose. At 10 o'clock, in correct dress, Kathleen went 'next door' to sing to the Queen who was staying there with her uncle. A friend wrote: 'Her Majesty sitting on a couch talking to Kath, who looked happy and quite at ease'. Kathleen closed the night with a brilliant piece of musical clowning which had everyone laughing; yet Kathleen was dying!

One last great flowering before fading. Sir John's great dream was *Orfeo* in English at Covent Garden. It was an open secret who was to be Orfeo. Meanwhile on 1st December she was informed that she had received the C.B.E. Of Kathleen in *Orfeo* Neville Cardus wrote:

Seldom has Covent Garden Opera House been so beautifully solemnised as when Kathleen Ferrier flooded the place with tone which seemed as though classic shapes in marble were changed into melody, warm, rich-throated, but chaste.

On the second performance, halfway through the second act, her leg seemed to give way. She sang on but the pain became unendurable. Yet after a rest in the wings she returned to sing the last aria—without a tremor. The applause rose. Flowers descended at her feet. The curtain fell. It was her public finale. She was taken from the dressing room to the hospital. Shortly after the Coronation she was informed that she had received the Gold Medal of the Royal Philharmonic Society, never awarded to a woman singer since 1914. On the 8th October, Coronation Year, Lancashire's greatest singer died.

Along with her singing she had a great range of interests. Entertaining, larking, painting, gardening, cooking, mucking-in in war-time, she tackled everything with a charm and grace which matched her genius, a genius that expressed itself alike in rollicking folk songs and in heart-rending lieder and oratorio—a great character and a great singer and to those that knew her and heard her an unforgettable memory.

Shortly before she died she sang to Sir John 'in a voice with all the bloom and tender ache of spring about it . . . the glory that was hers remained untouched'. Her last words to him were: 'goodbye, love'. An international star, but Lancashire to the last!

Sources and Further Reading

For the subjects of chapters 1–10 and chapter 12 there are entries in the *Dictionary of National Biography* (D.N.B.). Espinasse dealt with the subjects of chapter 1, 3, 4 and 5 in his *Lancashire Worthies*, Vol. I, and of chapter 6 and 7 in Vol. II. These writings are of much greater value in Vol. I than in Vol. II, which latter is now very scarce.

Chapter 1

18th and 19th century histories of the Derby earldom and Stanley family repeat certain traditions, without evaluation. *Cokayne's Complete Peerage*, Vols. IV and XII, gives a good factual outline of the first Earl's career, usefully supplementing D.N.B. The Stanely Poem, printed in *The Palatine Anthology* by J. O. Halliwell-Philips (1851), though full of legend, contains some arithmetic-sounding details. Professor A. R. Myer's writings, particularly his *English Historical Documents, 1327–1485*, and Dr R. L. Storey's *The Reign of Henry VII* help very much in elucidating the complex historical background. I thank Professor Myers and Eyre & Spottiswoode (Publishers) Ltd. for permission to quote from English Historical Documents, 1327–1485.

Chapter 2

John Foxe's *Book of Martyrs*, Vols. 7 and 8 is an uniquely valuable source-book, now fully vindicated by J. F. Mozley in *John Foxe and his Book*.

Chapter 3

The Life of Humphrey Chetham by Raines and Sutton (Chetham Society, 2nd series, Vols. 49 and 50) is valuable mainly for the documents it prints. Chetham's commercial significance is shown in Wadsworth and Manor's classic, *The Cotton Trade and Industrial Lancashire, 1600–1780* for permission to quote statistics from which I thank Miss Julie Mann and Manchester University Press.

Chapter 4

Although Wadsworth and Mann dealt with Arkwright, Dr R. Hills in *Richard Arkwright and Cotton Spinning* now expertly clarifies technical issues while Fitton & Wadsworth's *The Strutts and the Arkwrights* gives the full commercial setting. Thanks are due to Dr Hills and the Priory Press and Dr Fitton and the Manchester University Press respectively for permission to quote from these two works. Dr S. D. Chapman's *The Early Factory Masters* is also well worth reading.

Chapter 5

Hugh Malet's *The Canal Duke* and F. Mullineux' *The Duke of Bridgewater's Canal* (Eccles & District History Society pamphlet 1959), are both very good, readable works. I am indebted to Mr. Malet and to David & Charles Ltd, for permission to quote from his book.

Chapter 6

William Roscoe, by Dr G. Chandler is easily obtainable. There are a large number of articles which give more details of various aspects of Roscoe's life, of which Liverpool City Library has full bibliography. It also holds his original papers, while the Merseyside County Museums hold many of his relics and the Walker Art Gallery, Liverpool many of his pictures. Extremely important regarding Roscoe's political career is Ian Sellers' article 'William Roscoe, the Roscoe Circle and radical politics in Liverpool 1789–1807, (Trans. Hist. Soc. Lancs. & Ches. (T.H.S.L.C.), Vol. 120.)

Chapter 7

Professor C. Lloyd's *Mr. Barrow of the Admiralty* covers the subject well, but Barrow's printed autobiography gives fascinating details about Barrow's early life and local associations.

Chapter 8

Hugh Crow's fascinating memoirs have recently been reprinted.

Chapter 9

Mrs Gaskell's major works are now reprinted in Everyman's Library. Chapple & Pollard's edition of her *Letters*, with Dr McCready's article in T.H.S.L.C. Vol. 123 bring her to life. Miss A. B. Hopkins' *Elizabeth Gaskell, Her Life and Work* and Arthur Pollard's *Mrs Gaskell, Novelist & Biographer*, are good, scholarly but readable works. Dr E. Wright shows how critical opinion has recently changed in Mrs Gaskell's favour in *Mrs Gaskell, the Basis for Reassessment*. I acknowledge the permission of Harvard University Press for quoting the *Letters* and of Professor Asa Briggs and Penguin Books for the extract from *Frazer's Magazine* given in Professor Briggs' book *Victorian Cities*.

Chapter 10

The first volume of Professor Charles Wilson's *History of Unilever* and the *Life of the First Viscount Leverhulme* by his son, the 2nd Viscount, cover well the business and personal aspects of Lever's career. A sociological study of the Port Sunlight community is W. L. George, *Labour and Housing at Port Sunlight*. I am grateful to Professor Wilson and Cassell & Co. Ltd. and to the 3rd Viscount Leverhulme and George Allen & Unwin for permission to take quotations from the two above-mentioned books.

Chapter 11

Standard works are: M. Collis, *The Discovery of L. S. Lowry*, M. Levy, *L. S. Lowry* in *Painters of today* series (a Studio Book) and *Drawings of L. S. Lowry*. To these authors and to their publishers, Lund Humphries and Studio Vista, I tender thanks for permission to use extracts from their works. I am now also indebted to Barrie Stuart-Penrose, Nova Magazine, The North-West Arts Association, the Editor of the Guardian, Lord Clark, the Cultural Services Manager, City of Salford (for Monks Hall Museum, Eccles), Miss Carol Knock and the Director of the Walker Art Gallery, Liverpool.

Chapter 12

To Hamish Hamilton, publishers of Winifred Ferrier's readable and informative *Life of Kathleen Ferrier* and *Kathleen Ferrier, a Memoir*, I acknowledge my indebtedness and to Miss Ferrier, for permission to quote from the *Life*. C. Reid's and M. Kennedy's biographies of the late Sir John Barbirolli both contain an interesting chapter on Sir John's collaboration with Kathleen Ferrier. To M. Kennedy and his publishers, McGibbon and Kee, I am grateful also for permission to quote, also to the Editors of the *Guardian* and the *Musical Times*.